No fire, no thunder

No fire, no thunder

The threat of chemical
and biological weapons

Seán Murphy, Alastair Hay,
and Steven Rose

Monthly Review Press
New York

Library of Congress Cataloging in Publication Data
Murphy, Seán.
  No fire, no thunder.

  Includes index.
  1. Chemical warfare. 2. Biological warfare. I. Hay,
Alastair, 1947–   . II. Rose, Steven Peter Russell,
1938–   . III. Title.
UG447.M86   1984   358'.34   84-20579
ISBN 0-85345-661-5
ISBN 0-85345-662-3 (pbk.)

Monthly Review Press
155 West 23rd Street
New York, N.Y. 10011

Manufactured in the United States of America

10 9 8 7 6 5 4 3 2 1

For Ritchie Calder (1906–82),
lifelong campaigner against chemical weapons;

and for the women of Greenham, at the
forefront of today's struggle

Contents

Acknowledgements

Numerous people have helped and advised us, not only during the preparation of this book, but also in the three years since we initiated a campaign to draw attention to the threat of a new chemical arms race.

The Bertrand Russell Peace Foundation have supported our campaign. Julian Perry Robinson, of the Science Policy Research Unit at the University of Sussex, has been a source of comprehensive and reliable information; he continues as an unrivalled expert in this field and is a valued friend. Through END we have made contact with colleagues in other countries and through the Working Group on Chemical and Biological Weapons we have been able to communicate our concern in England. Dan Smith was responsible for suggesting that this book be written, and subsequently for sympathetically editing it. Valerie Shadbolt turned it into a manuscript and Wendy Hay grappled with the task of indexing.

We would especially like to thank the two thousand people – mainly laboratory scientists – who within the first few months of 1981 joined us in a single voice of alarm at the new threat of binary weapons. We hope that this book will provoke thousands more to do the same.

We three have worked closely together both before and during the preparation of this book, and although we each wrote separate sections, we take collective responsibility for the contents.

1. Chemical and biological weapons: the present threat

The arsenals of the superpowers are stocked to overflowing with nuclear-tipped missiles, capable of destroying the world's population many times over. Military strategists and their technicians are hard at work on a new generation of weapons, from neutron bombs to laser beams, and every effort of the nuclear disarmament movement is stretched to combat cruise, Trident and their fellows. At such a time it may seem self-indulgent, even a diversion, to raise the alarm concerning quite different types of weapon: chemical and biological. Haven't we got enough to worry about without thinking about these too?

Sadly, no. The military enthusiasm for new weaponry is insatiable. Along with the expansion of the nuclear arsenals, the last decades have seen a systematic development of all aspects of conventional weapons, from exotic new armour for tanks, through the fragmentation, vacuum and 'smart' bombs used with such effect by the Israelis in the battle for Beirut, to the electronic battlefield still on the drawing board (or rather the VDU) of the US military at the time of the collapse of their dreams in Saigon, but now in rapid production.

One of the most serious and sinister aspects of these new developments is the new escalation in research, development, production and stockpiling of chemical and biological weapons. Hidden behind the struggle of the Reagan administration over the MX missile project has been another battle over Reagan's demand for some $8 billion of expenditure over the period 1982–7 to develop a new generation of nerve gases, the so-called binary weapons: $0.7 billion was secured in 1982, and a further $1.0 billion authorised by Congress in 1983. Furthermore, at the back of the struggle over whether cruise missiles should be sited in Britain is the steady assumption by the US that Britain will also become the repository for stockpiles of these new nerve gases, packed into missile tips, bombs and shells, and intended for the European theatre of war.

A new chemical and biological weapons (CBW) arms race is under way. A few years ago the use of both types of weapons appeared to be precluded by the Geneva Protocol of 1925 – one of the oldest and apparently most successful of international arms control treaties. The Geneva Protocol had been buttressed by the Biological and Toxin Weapons Convention of 1972 which also banned development and stockpiling of these weapons. There was also slow and fitful progress towards a treaty on chemical weapons. Many of these gains seem to have been quietly eroded in the last few years, and we are on the verge of what may prove an irreversible escalation.

The scene has been set by what has been one of the most systematic disinformation campaigns of recent times. Over the past four years, scarcely a week has gone by without some scrap of news or rumour to contribute to a growing climate of fear. There are rumours of an increased Warsaw Pact chemical weapons build-up, based mainly on the evidence that Warsaw Pact forces have substantial CB decontamination units as part of their routine ground-force deployment. There are vigorously circulated stories of deaths from anthrax in the Russian town of Sverdlovsk, which the US says was the result of an accident or explosion at a biological warfare factory, and which the Soviet Union claims to have resulted from a conventional epidemic. Stories have circulated in the western press, allegedly based on reports from refugees, speaking of the Soviet use of chemical weaponry in Afghanistan. Eritrean sources claim that Soviet supplies of chemical weapons – conceivably nerve gas – have found their way into the hands of Ethiopian troops, and that there have been some gas attacks (just as the Palestinians claim that Israeli success in storming some of the more impregnable defence sites in Lebanon – notably Beaufort Castle – was achieved by the use of a knockout gas, possibly French in origin, which made the defenders temporarily unconscious).

Of course, the most persistent of the stories concerns the use of so-called 'yellow rain' by the Vietnamese or their Soviet supporters in Laos and Kampuchea. These reports began with accounts of seemingly unexplained deaths amongst refugees from Laos and Kampuchea – and particularly hill tribespeople. The deaths were often accompanied by extensive haemorrhage. Samples of leaves and twigs, taken from the area of alleged spraying for analysis in the US, showed high concentrations of toxins – poisonous, naturally occurring chemicals – derived from fungi (the so-called mycotoxins). In 1981 Alexander Haig used the occasion of a visit to Berlin to announce that the US had incontrovertible proof that these poisons were being sprayed in Indo-China; the next year the administration's spokesperson on these questions, Richard Burt, claimed that the US had 'the smoking gun' which clinched the argument. The use of such toxins would be a clear breach of the 1972 agreement. The Soviet Union and the Vietnamese have emphatically, indignantly and persistently denied the claims. Independent experts from the United Nations, from Canada, Australia and Britain – and from within the US – remain doubtful as to whether the gun is really smoking – and to whom it belongs anyhow. As we show later (in chapter 4) it is extremely difficult to see what military sense the use of such weapons by the Vietnamese would make.

But that isn't the point here. Allegations of the use of chemicals and biologicals by the Soviet Union and its allies have added to the climate of fear in which the undoubted reality of US chemical rearmament can be pressed forward. It is in this, above all, that the present danger lies.

Chemical and biological weapons have long fascinated military planners and science fiction writers. Silent and hidden killers, weapons of sabotage – LSD in the drinking water, a toxin in the ferrule of an umbrella to stab an unsuspecting enemy agent, a debilitating epidemic to weaken a hostile population, a pacifying gas that will make opposing troops lie on the ground in fits of helpless laughter while the goodies take control . . . fantasies have been rife. Even past generations of socialists have shared them, from novelist H.G.Wells to geneticist J.B.S. Haldane.

The truth, however, is somewhat different, as the chapters that follow show. First, there is no such thing as a non-lethal weapon. Chemical or biological poisons are only non-lethal if administered to healthy people in carefully controlled doses. There is no way in which a dose of an agent sufficient to immobilise *all* of an enemy force can be applied so as to avoid overdosing *some*. Substances which are relatively non-toxic at low doses to healthy 70-kilo soldiers are likely to be extremely harmful to the old, the young, the pregnant, the sick and the frail.

Second, even if the agents are *relatively* non-lethal, they have been used as an adjunct to more lethal weapons. An example is that of the irritant (tear gas) CS used by the US in Vietnam in the late 1960s and early 1970s. The US army field manual specifically spelt out the objective of using CS: to 'smoke out' guerillas from concealed tunnels and caves into the open, where they would come within the field of fire of such conventional weapons as napalm, phosphorus and fragmentation bombs.

There never has been a choice between 'gas and guns'. Where both exist, and military tactics dictate, you get both. Chemical and biological weapons are indiscriminate agents of mass destruction. Or, let us correct ourselves, they do indeed discriminate – they are *more* likely to kill non-combatants than combatants.

What is more, the very nature of the weapons means that they are likely to kill unpredictably and over a long period, with consequences – both military and civil – which cannot easily be assessed. An epidemic started by a biological warfare agent may take effect slowly and spread far beyond the boundaries of any war theatre, infecting even one's own troops. This uncertain military value is one reason, perhaps, why it was relatively easy to get agreement to a convention outlawing biological weapons, whereas chemicals have eluded control this past decade.

Things become even clearer when we move from the fantasy world of military 'scenario' writing to the world of fact. How, in reality, have chemical and biological weapons been used in the past? As chapter 2 describes, chemicals were first used in combat between the Germans and Allied troops during the First World War. They were used by one well-equipped military force against another to gain territory in bitterly contested trench warfare. There were hundreds of thousands of casualties. *This is the first and only time in the multitude of wars this century that chemical weapons have been used in this way.*

The entire subsequent history of the use of chemicals is quite different and reveals one overriding truth about these weapons. From the Italians against the Ethiopians to the Ethiopians against the Eritreans, from the Americans against the Vietnamese to, if true, the Vietnamese against the Laotians, the message is repeated. In each case chemicals have been used as the weapons of a technologically dominant, relatively well-equipped army and air force fighting relatively poorly-equipped rural guerillas. Above all, chemicals have been the weapons of imperialism, of the maintenance of technological hegemony.

Such a reality is extraordinarily at variance with the propaganda. If the militarily sensible way to use chemicals is by the US in Nicaragua and El Salvador, or by the USSR in Afghanistan, what are all those Soviet decontamination units doing in Eastern Europe? And why the immense pressure for a US build-up of a new generation of nerve gas weapons to be stockpiled in Western Europe?

In part, the pressure is the inexorable result of cold war logic, the if-you-have-them-we-must-too syndrome which underlies the name-calling and double-counting over cruise and SS20s. But it is more than mere macho posturing. In the US at least, Reagan's pressure to vote the money for the binary nerve gas programme is coming from a powerful Chemical Corps lobby. The US Chemical Corps has felt itself the poor relation in all the starwars wizardry of recent years, just as in the 1950s it felt so left out that it launched its own propaganda programme – 'Operation Blue Skies' – to encourage the US government into greater investment in chemical weapons research. That was the exercise which invented, for public consumption at least, the idea of a 'non-lethal' chemical agent, a sort of sanctioned psychedelic. And behind the US Chemical Corps, and hungry for orders, stands the giant US chemical industry looking for a way out of a recession. To some of that industry, $8 billion spent on new plant to make the binary weapons, and on inactivating old stock, is money worth playing for.

The danger is that we become the victims of the make-believe; that all those military exercises on Salisbury Plain, complete with troops in their CBW protective clothing, become a taken-for-granted part of the scenery; that we acquiesce in this new spiral to the arms race. As our book is designed to show, this danger is not merely of the present and the next generation of chemical and biological weapons, horrific though such a prospect might be. Already waiting in the laboratories, under contract from the military here and in the US – and doubtless in the Soviet Union too – are future generations of these weapons, made possible by the breakthroughs in biological research and its industrialisation which go by the names of 'biotechnology' and 'genetic engineering'.

In September 1983 the US House of Representatives ended a 15-year moratorium on the production of nerve gas when, by a vote of 266 to 152, it authorised the $187.5 billion defence bill for 1984. While the House had, in June, voted against providing money for the production of binary weapons the Senate, in July, voted for it, though only after Vice President Bush bust a tie-breaker of 49 for and 49 against. This about-face in the House was the result of a number of factors, not the least being the destruction of the South Korean airline's Boeing 747 by a Soviet air-defence fighter plane.

It is not yet too late to stop these developments. But time is not on our side: we have only determination and the belief which the women of Greenham Common have shown us all that it is possible to roll back technology by human struggle. Our book is intended as a tool in that struggle.

2. Chemical weapons

Early days: mustard, phosgene, Lewisite and hydrogen cyanide

Confrontation in Europe in the early part of this century provided testing grounds for new generations of weapons and for new ways to deliver them. Trench warfare and cavalry attacks passed into history. Tanks enabled breakthrough attacks against the front line. Immune to machine-gun fire and the treacherous barbed wire, they ploughed across dug-outs with impunity. Land artillery gave way to aerial bombardment. Unheard and mostly unseen, waves of gas enveloped friend and foe alike; crude incendiaries gave birth to napalm. These were weapons designed to incapacitate, to wound, to kill. The age of modern warfare had begun.

Earlier custom had condemned the use in war of weapons believed to cause unnecessary suffering, including poison weapons. The Brussels Convention of 1874 and the Hague Declaration of 1899 prohibited 'the use of projectiles, the object of which is the diffusion of asphyxiating or deleterious gases'.[1] These flimsy agreements were set aside when, one day in April 1915, German Pioneers opened the valves of thousands of cylinders of liquid chlorine along a four-mile front near Ypres – after all, *projectiles* were not being used to disseminate the gas. Such cynicism about the wording of agreements, or their total disregard, has become commonplace in the history of the use of chemical weapons. Today, a major stumbling-block in the way of a comprehensive chemical weapons treaty is the precise definition of the weapons that should be included.

The 1914–18 war was the first experiment on a large scale in the use of chemical weapons. Some five months after the Ypres experience the British retaliated – again with chlorine. In December of 1915, again at Ypres, the Germans used phosgene for the first time. The British retaliated with a mixture of chlorine and phosgene. The Germans developed the first tear gas (T-Stoff, named after a Dr *T*appen) for use on the Russian front in 1915. The French were experimenting with hydrogen cyanide. Laboratories in England tested 150,000 known chemicals in an attempt to develop the most lethal gas. Any pretence to abide by the Hague Declaration was abandoned in 1917 when gas shells were first used by the Germans. These were filled with a brown liquid – dichlorethyl sulphide – that came to be known as mustard gas. The persistence of this agent, and its effects, were such that in a few months the number of British casualties reached 125,000, 70 per cent of the total British gas casualties for the whole war. The British and French developed their own mustard gas in response. A huge US research effort culminated in Lewisite, which produced similar effects but faster.

The devastating effects of these agents (see Table 1, p. 111) during this war were the result of surprise, novelty and lack of preparedness. Phosgene and chlorine, both lung irritants, stripped the lining of the air passages. The irritation resulted in massive secretion of fluid into the airways, blocking the lungs and the windpipe. Those exposed drowned in their own mucus. Phosgene was superior to chlorine because it was invisible, had little odour, was effective at lower concentration and had a delayed action. All these gases were effective only if breathed and respirators were soon developed to protect the troops. The response to these protective measures was the introduction of an agent with a different mode of action. Mustard gas is a vesicant, that is, it causes blistering of the skin. British troops did not bother to put on their gas masks when first exposed to mustard gas, feeling only a slight irritation to the eyes and throat. After some hours the irritation gave way to excruciating pain, relieved only by morphia. Mustard gas lay around on the ground, contaminating clothing and equipment. The blistering was extensive and death resulted from congestion of the lungs. To survive, not only masks but full protective clothing had to be worn and decontamination of all surfaces had to become a routine practice.

This experience of the use of gas horrified the civilian population of the countries involved. Over one million men on all sides had been wounded by gas between 1915 and 1918 and some 10 per cent of these casualties were fatal.[2] However, the furious research endeavour in the laboratories of the major protagonists had opened a box filled with horrors. The French, Americans and British learned much from developments in the German chemical industries after the armistice of 1918. Research into novel chemical agents continued – in Britain, secretly; and in the USA, quite openly. Here then was a dilemma. Gas had horrified and yet fascinated military commanders. Chemical weapons had proved to be of some military value in a major war, judged by the number of casualties.

Two more opportunities for testing chemical agents presented themselves to British commanders. During the Russian civil war that followed the 1917 Revolution, British, French and US governments intervened in an attempt to break the new Bolshevik government. In 1919 British planes dropped canisters which produced clouds of arsenic smoke into the forests around Archangel and also supplied the White army with gas shells. Later that year, phosgene and mustard gas were repeatedly used by the RAF against Afghanis and hill tribespeople on the north-west frontier.[3]

Between 1919 and 1925 there were numerous attempts under the auspices of the League of Nations to formulate a comprehensive treaty to ban chemical weapons.[4] These resulted in the 1925 Geneva Protocol which banned the first use in war of chemical and bacteriological agents. In some ways this was a milestone, but the Protocol has many flaws. First, though nearly 40 countries signed it,[5] some (e.g. the USA) took 50 years to ratify their signatures. Second, the Protocol banned *first* use: thus a country could reserve the right to retaliate in kind if attacked.[6] Third, the Protocol did not affect countries which were not signatories. Fourth, the scope of the provisions was not clear. Were tear gases included? What about incendiary weapons? And later there were defoliants. Lastly, the Protocol did not ban research into development and stockpiling of chemical weapons.

Between 1925 and 1945 many countries pursued research into

novel chemical agents and there were opportunities to test these agents in numerous locations. The principal countries involved were Britain, USA, Japan, France, Soviet Union, Italy and Germany. Research was carried out in several establishments such as that at Porton Down, Wiltshire (set up in 1916, it is now the Chemical Defence Establishment); Edgewood Arsenal, Maryland, USA; and Tandanoumi Arsenal, Japan.

The first major breach of the Geneva Protocol happened in 1935–6 when Italian aircraft sprayed phosgene, tear and mustard gases over vast areas of Ethiopia during their attempts to annex the country.[7] Both countries were party to the Geneva Protocol. Italy did not explicitly deny the allegations, but accused the Ethiopians of having violated the established rules of conduct in war, so justifying Italian use of poison gas. The League of Nations tried to apply economic and financial sanctions against Italy, but these were half-hearted and were never extended to include military measures. They failed to stop the aggression and the use of chemical weapons. In 1938 poison gas (Lewisite and mustard) was also alleged to have been used by Japanese forces on the Shantung front in China. China, but not Japan, had ratified the Geneva Protocol. The documentary evidence[8] was not as clear as that in Ethiopia – nevertheless, apart from reservations expressed by the British delegation, the Council of the League of Nations had few doubts that gas had been employed. However, with the rapid development of events in Europe at this time the attention of the League of Nations was elsewhere.

The fruits of chemical weapons research between 1919 and 1939 were two-fold. First, sophisticated means had been devised to deliver chemical agents such as mustard, phosgene, Lewisite and hydrogen cyanide, the lung irritants and blood and blister gases of 1914–18 vintage (Table 1, p. 111). Second, and most significantly, a new class of chemical agent had been discovered – nerve gas.

German developments: the nerve gases

Research into novel forms of insecticide in Germany in the giant I.G.Farben chemical company (later to produce Zyklon B – the gas used to kill hundreds of thousands in the gas chambers of the concentration camps) led to a consideration of organophosphorus compounds. In 1936 Gerhard Schrader at IGF discovered a compound that killed insects but also had highly undesirable effects on humans; he named it 'tabun'. Though of little use as an insecticide it had military potential and intensive research followed. Tabun exerted its effects in novel and militarily useful ways. Unlike the other poison gases, tabun could also enter the body through the skin by absorption. Its effects were very specific: it disrupted the function of the nervous system by inhibiting a key enzyme – acetylcholinesterase.

Muscular contraction is initiated in many species of animals, including ourselves, by the release of a chemical substance from the nerve fibres that run to the muscles. This chemical substance is acetylcholine and there are specific patches of membrane on each muscle that are receptive to it. The acetylcholine binds to the muscle, altering its electrical state and hence causing it to contract. Muscles do not exist in a permanent state of contraction because they also contain an enzyme, acetylcholinesterase, which breaks down the acetylcholine released from the nerve fibres – in this way, the muscle may relax once more. If this enzyme is prevented from working then the muscle goes into a state of spasm and cannot be relaxed. Probably the most important muscles are those of the heart and of the rib cage, for the latter control the filling and emptying of the lungs. If the inhibition of the enzyme is not reversible then the only possibility for recovery of muscle function is by the production of more enzyme by the body – a process which takes hours or days. Tabun is an *irreversible* inhibitor of acetylcholinesterase. It is 100–1,000 times more toxic than chlorine and 10–100 times more potent than mustard gas, phosgene, Lewisite or hydrogen cyanide (see Table 2, p. 114). A few thousandths of a gram (enough to cover a pinhead) prove fatal, the immediate cause of death being asphyxiation.

A year later Schrader discovered a compound similar to tabun which was ten times more toxic. He named this 'sarin' after the four key individuals involved in its production (*S*chrader, *A*mbros, *R*udriger and van der *Lin*de). The Wehrmacht poured over a hundred million marks into the building of a nerve gas factory near Breslau in Silesia.[9] Its monthly capacity was 3,000 tons of tabun and aircraft bombs and shells were filled with the liquid compound in a vast underground plant. In 1944 a third compound, related to the other two but more lethal (see Table 2), was discovered and named 'soman'. By this time Germany had a score of factories capable of producing 10,000 tons of poison gas each month. In addition to tabun and a small amount of sarin, mustard gas and phosgene were produced on a large scale. Estimates of stockpiles by the end of the war varied from 70,000 to 250,000 tons.[10]

Though the secret of *nerve* gas was well kept by the Germans (Allied commanders had no idea of these developments) production of *poison* gas had not lagged behind in Britain and the US. By 1945 5,000,000 tons of poison gas had been stockpiled, principally mustard and phosgene. These were manufactured at plants near Runcorn in Cheshire, and in Clwyd. US-produced poison gas started to arrive in Britain from 1940.[11] Many new chemical warfare plants were built in the US between 1942 and 1945. The largest was at Pine Bluff in Arkansas. In the 1980s this plant is a new focus for poison gas production.

Expenditure on poison gas of all sorts on all sides during the 1939–45 war was immense. Repeatedly, the prospect of using poison gas seemed likely during this time. Churchill seemed particularly fascinated by the idea. For one reason or another, though, it never happened.[12] Hitler was convinced that the Allied forces knew about, and had produced, nerve gas and therefore was reluctant to initiate gas attacks. By the time it seemed inevitable (1944), the Luftwaffe had too few aircraft left to deliver the payload. Remarkably, poison gas was not employed in Europe during this period and only on one front in Asia (by the Japanese against the Chinese). The reasons for this are diverse and make fascinating reading.[13]

Second World War to cold war: escalation

Captured Japanese and German stocks of chemical munitions were mostly dumped in the various seas of the world. However, the supplies of nerve gas, the production factories and the technicians running them were very useful catches. The tabun and sarin plants fell into Soviet hands almost intact – and with them the documents relating to the most recent discovery, soman. Supposedly, these factories were dismantled and rebuilt on the banks of the Volga.[14] Many of the scientific staff of these factories were captured by the Americans and British and the secret of nerve gas was revealed to the victorious Allies.

The uneasy political unity between the Allies broke down finally in 1945. The Soviet Union saw the threat of the atomic weapons developed in America by a multinational group of scientists and experimentally tested in Japan. The West recognised the chemical weapons potential that the Soviet Union had suddenly gained. Far from winding down the production of poison and nerve gas, the period between 1945 and 1969 saw a continuing investment in these weapons, coupled with developments in biological agents.

One new development occurred in the 1950s, the discovery of the V agents. Schrader's discovery of the G agents (tabun, sarin and soman) was as interesting to insecticide manufacturers as to the military, and organophosphorus research proceeded at a great pace. During 1952 and 1953 three chemical firms discovered a group of compounds particularly effective against mites.[15] Schrader (still working in Germany and now with the company Bayer), Tammelin in Sweden and Ghosh at ICI in England modified these compounds. Ghosh's work was taken up by the Chemical Defence Establishment at Porton Down and similar establishments in the USA were notified at the same time. One of these compounds, code-named VX, was selected for large-scale manufacture. A factory was constructed in the US in 1959, production began in 1961, and tens of thousands of tons of VX were produced before production ceased in 1969.

VX is the most toxic nerve gas yet produced. It is some ten times more effective than soman (see Table 2, p.114) and the skin is very permeable to it. Unlike the other nerve gases, VX is an oily liquid with a high viscosity. This makes it a very persistent agent, which can lie around for up to three weeks if the weather is warm with little wind or for up to sixteen weeks at −10°C in calm weather.

While Britain destroyed most of its stocks of captured and manufactured poison gas in the late 1950s,[16] France, America and the Soviet Union continued production. US production stopped in 1969,[17] and there is no hard evidence of any production by the Soviet Union since that time. France had a nerve gas production plant at Toulouse which operated from 1965 to 1974. Currently these three are the only countries known to possess stocks of poison and nerve gas.[18] France is suspected of having some hundreds of tons of nerve gas. We have to rely on US estimates for information about Soviet stocks as Soviet officials have made little direct public reference to the existence of such weapons since 1938. The US has no firm information about the size of the Soviet stockpile. Estimates vary from 30,000 to 700,000 tons, but the latter figure is considered by many to be implausibly high. A West German estimate suggests 20,000–70,000 tons, the agents being phosgene, mustard, hydrogen cyanide plus the nerve gases tabun and soman.[19]

Much more is known of the US stockpile of poison gas.[20] It amounts to 42,000 tons, about half of which is mustard gas either left over from production in the 1940s or the result of a programme of production between 1952 and 1959. The other half is in the form of nerve gas in two varieties: sarin (more than 70 per cent) produced between 1952 and 1959 and VX produced between 1961 and 1967.

Over half of the poison gas is stored in bulk, in one-ton containers, while the remainder is loaded into weapons. While 90 per cent of stocks are held in domestic depots and arsenals (the bulk at Tooele Army Depot, Utah; Pine Bluff, Arkansas; and Umatilla Army Depot, Oregon), two foreign locations are known. The first is on Johnston Island in the Pacific. Stocks here amount to 5 per cent of the total stockpile in the form of mustard, sarin and VX. This material was originally at the US base on the Japanese Island of Okinawa, but the Pentagon ordered its transfer in 1971 when VX was found to be leaking from a container and a number of servicemen were affected. The second overseas dump of nerve gas is in West Germany and comprises 2–5 per cent of the total US poison gas stockpile. It is reported to be held at a single location, at Fischbach near Pirmasens, though unconfirmed reports suggest as many as five locations. (The US has over 30 ammunition supply points in the Federal Republic.) The poison gas stock is not assigned to NATO and remains totally under US control.

Use, propaganda and the 'binary' system

Since 1945 there have been numerous reports of the use of poison gas in warfare. The first were in Korea and China in the early 1950s where the allegations included the use, by the US, of biological agents (see chapter 3).[21] In May 1951 B-29 aircraft, it was claimed, attacked the city of Nampo (North Korea) with gas bombs. A thousand people were affected and nearly 50 per cent died of suffocation. Again in July, August and in January of the next year, US planes were said to have spread gas in Won San and in Hwanghai. The UN disarmament commission, the Security Council and the General Assembly considered the charges in 1952 and 1953. The US naturally denied the allegations but the Soviet proposal to invite representatives of the People's Republic of China and the People's Democratic Republic of Korea to participate in the discussions was rejected. The majority of UN members considered the evidence unconvincing, but US proposals for impartial investigation were rejected by the accusers. The US at this time had still not ratified the Geneva Protocol of 1925 and was reluctant to do so, apparently because it feared that such a move might precipitate a move to ban nuclear weapons as well.

During the 1963–7 civil war in the Yemen between the royalist regime (backed by Saudi Arabia) and the republican authorities (backed by Egypt), allegations were made that lethal gas was used by Egyptian forces.[22] It was alleged that gas had killed people and animals by asphyxiation in Kitaf (Northern Yemen) on 5 January 1967. The then British prime minister, Harold Wilson, repeated these allegations in the House of Commons. Egypt responded by inviting a UN fact-finding mission to the Yemen. The Red Cross had issued a statement confirming Egypt's use of poison gas, but no action was taken by the United Nations. The reason for this was the general crisis situation in the Middle

East, many governments having overriding reasons of national interest not to get involved in claim and counter-claim. The war in Yemen gave way to the Arab–Israeli war. The type and source of the agent were never discovered. Although there were claims of nerve gas it was probably mustard gas that was used. There are suggestions that the source was British – old stocks buried in the desert in the 1940s and dug up by the Egyptians.

In the last 10 years, there have been allegations of poison gas being used in Laos (by Laotian and Vietnamese forces, since 1974), in Kampuchea (by Vietnamese forces, since 1978), in Angola (by South African air forces, May 1978), in Vietnam (by Vietnamese and Chinese forces against each other, in 1979), in Afghanistan (by Soviet and Mujahideen forces against each other, since 1979), in Ethiopia (by Ethiopian forces, since 1980), in Iran and Iraq (by Iraqi and Iranian forces, since 1980), in El Salvador (by Salvadorean Army and National Guard, since 1981), in the Lebanon (by Israeli forces, 1982) and in Thailand (by Vietnamese forces, 1982).[23] These reports vary in their credibility. Because of their implications for East–West relations, the reports relating to Afghanistan, Kampuchea and Laos have attracted the widest attention. To date, no conclusive evidence has been presented to substantiate any of these claims of use of poison gas. The allegations of use of biological weapons are covered in chapters 3 and 4.

One reason for the recent flood of allegations concerning use of both chemical and biological agents is the obvious intention of the US to begin a programme of gas production and re-equipping of its troops.[24] At the instigation of President Nixon, US production of poison gas was halted in 1969, and the 1970s saw productive disarmament negotiations. However, the chemical warfare lobby in the various US administrations since then has been growing. The US has, each year, committed money to a CW defence programme. However, in 1980 it became clear that a long-term programme had been planned to replace old stocks of poison gas with new agents. First, money was voted for a new plant at the Pine Bluff Arsenal, then the money for equipment was approved. In 1982, President Reagan requested money for the production of nerve gas but was denied it by Congress.

Again, in 1983, the budget request contained items for the production of nerve gas – and this time, after much debate in Congress, the request was approved.

The cessation of poison gas production in the US in 1969 was the result of many pressures. These came from NATO allies reluctant to house it, from the anti-Vietnam war lobby and from the environmental lobby in the US (poison gas is just too dangerous to ship around). There had been accidents. In March 1968, VX leaked from a container on an F4 Phantom jet that had been test spraying at Dugway Proving Ground, Utah. The nerve gas was carried by the wind out of the designated area and finally settled 20 miles away. The victims were thousands of sheep.

In the 1970s, however, research by the Chemical Corps came up with an answer – the 'binary' weapon. While 50 per cent of the US gas stockpile is in the form of bulk storage containers, the remainder is 'weaponised' in various munitions. The chemical agents themselves do not deteriorate significantly upon storage but the filled munitions do deteriorate over the years to the point of unserviceability – indeed, some are now obsolete, as the weapon systems for which they were designed have since been overtaken by new models. Perhaps one-third of US stocks are therefore presently unusable – now would be the time to replace them.[25] To overcome the problems associated with manufacturing, storing and distributing extremely lethal chemical agents such as nerve gas, the plan is to produce two less toxic chemical substances and load them separately into the munition. This is the binary idea.

Binaries introduce a new dimension into the possibility of chemical warfare. The need for high security/high technology chemical plant recedes. Any country with an advanced chemical industry could manufacture one or both of the components. Verification procedures, in the advent of a disarmament treaty, would be made very difficult indeed.

The proposed binary weapons are a means to deliver the same agents (sarin, soman and VX) but in a different way. For example, an artillery shell would have the space for two canisters, one containing isopropanol, the other methyl phosphonyl difluoride. One of the two canisters would be loaded into the shell which could then be shipped reasonably safely. The second canister would be shipped and stored separately, and loaded just before firing the shell. A disc separating the two canisters would be ruptured either by the velocity of the projectile or by a small delay charge. The contents of the two canisters would mix in the shell in flight and the impact of the shell, or a mid-air explosion, would release the contents – sarin.[26] The military drawback is that only 70 per cent of the payload would end up as nerve gas. The advantages, again in military terms, are safety for ground crew, improved dispersal and easier disposal if necessary. All G and V agents are capable of being made in this way. In the US some 15 types of munitions are being developed in the binary mode.[27] The first planned are a 155mm artillery shell, a spray-bomb (Bigeye) for F-111 aircraft, and rocket warheads for a multiple rocket launcher which is a joint venture between the US, Britain, West Germany and France. France is thought to be developing binary nerve gas technology at its factory at Toulouse.[28] It would be surprising if the technology was not also well advanced in the Soviet Union.

As well as poison gas . . .

So far, we have focused on one category of chemical weapon – poison gas. The agents in this category are classified by the military as being lethal, anti-personnel agents. But the arsenal contains others. These are harassing agents (tear gas), incapacitating agents (psychochemicals), anti-plant chemicals (defoliants) and incendiary weapons. Whether all, some or none of these are covered by the 1925 Geneva Protocol is a moot point. That they are all horrendous weapons is beyond doubt.

'Harassing agents' are defined as chemical compounds capable of causing a rapid but temporary disablement, lasting little longer than the period of exposure. These are stockpiled and used routinely by military and internal security forces across the world. Whether or not the use of tear gas was covered by the Geneva Protocol first became controversial in 1930 when the British delegation stated that, in its view, use of the gas in war was prohibited. The only dissenting note came from the US representative who argued that these agents had a humane purpose and were, in any case, used in peacetime to control civilian populations.[29] The first tear gas was developed in the US in 1918, and code-named CN (see Table 1, p. 111). Dispersed as an aerosol, CN is active at a concentration of less than one-thousandth of a gram (1mg) per cubic metre of air breathed. The chemical's properties are outlined in the 1966 US military manual:

CN quickly irritates the upper respiratory passages and eyes, causing an intense flow of tears within seconds. As a secondary effect, in high concentrations, CN is irritating to the skin and can cause a burning, itching sensation, especially on moist parts of the body. Some individuals experience nausea.[30]

CN is also lethal on exposure for 10 minutes to an airborne density of less than a gram per cubic metre and several civilians have died from CN-poisoning through 'improper' use.

Many police departments now favour CS (see Table 1, p. 111), developed at Porton Down in the 1950s and named after its original American discoverers, Carson and Stoughton. It is fired as a shell or cartridge and dispersed as an aerosol or dust which irritates the eyes, nose and throat causing a gripping pain in the chest. CS is part of the armoury of British troops and police. It has been used frequently in France, Poland, the US and Northern Ireland and was used in Liverpool (in 1981) to near lethal effect. Though CS is less toxic than CN it affects more body systems and undoubtedly can kill, especially if those exposed are in a confined space and cannot escape, or are young, old or sick. The newest of the tear gases is CR (see Table 1, p. 111), discovered at Salford Technical College (now Salford University) in the 1960s, and adopted for use by the US army in 1972 and the British Ministry of Defence in 1973. It can be fired in cartridges or, as it is water soluble, from water cannons. One of its effects is claimed to be to generate hysteria.

The most consistent use of tear gas was by the US in Vietnam. The proliferation of CS munitions for every conceivable delivery system was staggering. Not just hand and rifle grenades, but munitions for mortar, cannon, rocket launchers, aircraft and helicopters. CS was not used for crowd control, but to force Viet-

namese out of particular areas – be they small tunnels or square
miles of open ground. A lasting form of CS powder was dusted
onto the ground so that anyone passing across it created a cloud
of intolerable irritant. CS in this form is very persistent, lasting for
up to two weeks. Many died in Vietnam, either as a direct result
of exposure to tear gas or because the agent was used to drive
them out into the open where they were killed by 'conventional'
weapons.

The legal position on the use of tear gases remains equivocal.
Both Britain and the US maintain that CS is not covered by the 1925
Protocol. In a recent hearing before the Committee on Foreign
Affairs in the US House of Representatives, Michael Matheson
(Assistant Legal Adviser for Political Military Affairs, State
Department) was examined by Congressman Stephen Solarz:

> *Solarz:* Our position is even though we formally ratified the
> [1925 Geneva] convention, we consider the use of the
> weapons we used in Viet Nam to be compatible with the
> requirements of that convention?
> *Matheson:* Yes.
> *Solarz:* Why?
> *Matheson:* We have interpreted the prohibition . . . as not
> applying to irritant gases in use in *domestic* circumstances.
> *Solarz:* Is this . . . broadly accepted in the international legal
> community?
> *Matheson:* It is not the majority view.[31]

Note the use of the term 'domestic'. Vietnam, it seems,
became, for a time, the fifty-first state of the Union.

Nerve gases have effects on many parts of the nervous system.
A number of compounds are found naturally, or can be synthe-
sised, that *stimulate* or *block* specific nerve pathways. Such
compounds form the basis for much of today's drug therapy, but
their usefulness as weapons has not escaped the military. If the
compounds block or stimulate key nerve pathways in the brain or
spinal cord, then they will incapacitate the victim for a period of
time before being degraded by the body (the toxins dealt with
in chapter 3 have similar sites of action, but are often lethal in
their effects). The US Army's interest in these psychochemicals

was stimulated by the rapid development of psychotropic drugs by pharmaceutical companies after 1945. By 1952, the Chemical Corps had contracts out (e.g. with Shell) to find useful agents.[32] Lysergic acid diethylamide (LSD) and tetrahydrocannabinol (an active ingredient of cannabis resin) were among thousands that were screened. The idea was to produce non-lethal incapacitating agents in contrast to the very toxic poison gases. 'Operation Blue Skies' was launched by the US Chemical Corps as a publicity drive to win support for its mission. Psychochemicals were introduced as 'humane' weapons which would, temporarily, disable enemy forces without doing lasting harm, enabling a peaceful US takeover.

In 1962, the US Army was in the process of erecting a manufacturing plant for incapacitating-agent weapons. The agent involved was code-named BZ (see Table 1, p. 111). This is a psychotropic agent which blocks particular nerve pathways that utilise acetylcholine as a transmitter, especially the nerves to the heart and in those parts of the brain involved with the control of movement. The symptoms of BZ poisoning are rapid heart rate, blurred vision, loss of co-ordination and amnesia. The US currently holds a 50-ton stockpile of BZ at Pine Bluff Arsenal, though it is not at all clear how effective such agents would be as weapons.[33] The only extensive field 'experiment' involving psychedelics in war was the large-scale (voluntary) taking of drugs such as cannabis and heroin by US troops in Vietnam. Such practices did not noticeably detract from their military aggressiveness. The other point is that the idea of a non-lethal incapacitant is untenable. Doses that will render some people incapable will prove fatal to others, depending upon their state of health.

The Central Intelligence Agency (CIA) had a particular interest in the use of psychochemicals to control human behaviour. It began in the 1950s in a search for drugs that would wipe out the memory of 'spent' undercover agents and defectors. Known drug addicts (mostly black males) were used in trials with LSD. There were reports of cannabis and LSD being given to unsuspecting victims, at least one of whom died.[34] With the advent of the US Freedom of Information Act in 1981, the full extent of these CIA research projects became publicly known.

The control of vegetation by herbicides is not novel. When plant hormones were first identified and purified in the 1920s it became clear that specific hormones control growth. In large amounts these substances cause abnormal growth and plants outgrow their strength. Investigations into the military use of herbicides as crop-destruction agents began in England in 1940, and it was the British who were the first to use herbicides in a military conflict. During the Malayan Emergency, which persisted from 1948 to 1958, British forces used the herbicide 2,4,5-T against the Communist insurgents to control vegetation along lines of communication and to destroy food crops. But it was in the Vietnam war that herbicides and anti-crop chemicals were used on a large scale. Some 17 million gallons of mixtures (e.g. Agents Orange, Blue, White) of 2,4-D (used in lawns for weed-killing), 2,4,5-T, picloram and cacodylate (an arsenic chemical) (see Table 1, p. 113) were sprayed by a US Air Force squadron, boasting the slogan 'Only we can prevent forests.'[35] Between 1962 and 1971, US scientists estimate that 10 per cent of the country's inland forests, 36 per cent of the mangrove forests, 3 per cent of cultivated land and 5 per cent of 'other' land was affected.[36]

The defoliation programme was initially described as part of the strategy of denying forest cover to the guerillas in largely jungle terrain. However, one important aspect of this was the destruction of crops. The grand US strategy was to drive the largely agrarian, peasant population into the towns or strategic hamlets – vast concentration camps, where the availability of food could be effectively controlled by the US and its puppet government in Saigon. The weapons soon became responsible for large-scale starvation. Had this been the only effect of the spraying it would have been serious enough. However, before long it became clear that animals and humans were being directly affected by exposure to aircraft-spraying of the defoliants. There were reports of death, of cancers and birth abnormalities. One reason for these human casualties was that Agent Orange (a 1:1 mixture of 2,4,5-T and 2,4-D) was heavily contaminated with dioxin, a very stable toxic compound now known to cause birth abnormalities and cancer in animals.[37] Dioxin is produced as an impurity during the manufacture of 2,4,5-T and its danger to humans only became widely recognised in Europe when contamination of people and land followed factory explosions during production – at Coalite, Derbyshire, in 1968; and Seveso, Italy, in 1976. It is estimated that 170kg of dioxin was accidentally sprayed on Vietnam, Laos and Cambodia (Kampuchea) during the war.[38] Dioxin is more toxic than nerve gas and a few grams would be sufficient to wipe out a population the size of London.

Twelve years after the spraying finished, Vietnam's inland forests still bear the scars. Despite a massive replanting programme begun in 1977 around Ho Chi Minh City, Vietnamese scientists are convinced that defoliation has led to changes in local rainfall, excessive erosion and irreparable damage to the local fauna and flora. Of equal concern are the effects of the spraying on people. Vietnamese scientists have evidence of an increase in liver cancer, spontaneous abortion and birth defects.[39] In addition, 23,000 US, Australian, Korean and New Zealand servicemen have collectively sued the five chemical companies which manufactured the defoliants, claiming that their health has been irreparably damaged.[40]

'Incendiary weapons', like the irritant agents, are commonplace in military arsenals. While not positively covered by the 1925 Geneva Protocol they were – until 1939 – generally regarded as illegal and inhumane, in the same category as weapons such as mustard gas. During the 1939–45 war illegality was ignored and a well-defined policy of incendiary bombing emerged – the destruction of Dresden by the RAF, Tokyo by the USAF, Coventry by the Luftwaffe. This practice converted hitherto unconventional into conventional weapons, a path along which the poison gases are now in danger of running.

Incendiaries have been a standard weapon of war since 1945, most horrifically in South-East Asia between 1961 and 1975.[41] In the 10-year period 1963–73 the US dropped 388,000 tons of napalm bombs in Indo-China, 10 per cent of the total fighter-bomber munitions used. Napalm, a US invention of the late 1930s, is a mixture of fuel (e.g. aviation fuel or paraffin) and thickening agent (e.g. rubber or polystyrene) to increase the burning time.[42] The thickened oil spreads out on the ground, increasing the chances of igniting anything combustible around it. Phosphorus is added to the mixture to cause ignition and high temperatures (800–1,000°C). Burning napalm is difficult to extinguish and smoke-generating compounds (e.g. benzene) can be added to prevent even an attempt.

In addition to napalm, magnesium and white phosphorus incendiary cluster bombs were used in Vietnam (and more recently by the Israelis in Lebanon). These compounds ignite spontaneously in air. Incendiaries were used in Vietnam in the same way as defoliants and irritants – to deny areas to the guerillas and in search-and-destroy operations. As the caricatured American colonel reflects, nostalgically, after a bombing raid on a small coastal fishing village in South Vietnam in Francis Ford Coppola's film *Apocalypse Now*, 'I love the smell of napalm in the morning . . . It smells like . . . victory!'

Despite the hundreds of thousands of tons of incendiaries and the thousands of Vietnamese dead from shock, asphyxiation (oxygen is removed from the air) and infection after burns, there was no victory for the Americans.

In 1972, 99 nations of the UN General Assembly voted in favour (and none against) a resolution deploring the use of napalm and other incendiaries in armed conflicts (15 nations abstained including France, Britain and the USA). Again in 1974, 98 nations of the General Assembly voted in favour of a resolution calling upon states to refrain from production, stockpiling and proliferation of incendiary weapons (27 nations abstained including France, the USSR, Britain and the USA).[43] It remains to be written into international law.

This chapter has shown that three countries – the USA, USSR and France – possess stocks of some of the most toxic chemicals so far discovered, and in a form designed for warfare. The nerve gases, if ever used, will destroy soldiers and civilians alike. In addition, because these chemical agents act directly on the nervous system, many species of animals would be affected. If the ecology of an area were disrupted in this way, there would be devastating consequences for all animal and plant populations. What happened in Vietnam in the 1960s and 1970s would be magnified many times in Europe.

Attention is currently focused on the more obvious weapons of mass destruction. The British and, subsequently, US and Russian policies not to continue production of chemical agents have lulled us into a false sense of security. Waiting just off-stage have been the new binary weapons – and now they have emerged into the spotlight. These weapons, brought in by the US as a bargaining chip in the disarmament negotiations, will destroy or slacken the progress made at Geneva.

The chemical agents described are the products of 70 years of military exploitation of scientific research. Similarly, the military have been quick to see the potential in the rapid progress in biological research, adding to their arsenal for waging war the even more potent biological and toxin agents.

3. Biological weapons

The prospect of bombs filled with infectious diseases is a horrific one to many people: not unnaturally they abhor the idea that infections might be spread deliberately as a means of waging war. Whatever we feel about the subject, this is indeed what biological weapons are all about. They are bacteria, viruses, fungi or rickettsia (a form of bacteria) which are used in wartime to cause disease or death in people. Some bacteria are so toxic that an initial small dose can be lethal. In other cases, and particularly with viruses, the disease results from the infectious agent multiplying inside the host cell and destroying it before moving on to new cells. Eventually, the virus overwhelms the body's defensive mechanisms. Viruses are not viable on their own; they need to grow inside other cells. Bacteria, on the other hand, are viable and require only a source of food for growth. Viruses are toxic in their own right, but in the case of bacteria it is usually the toxins they produce which are dangerous: *Clostridium botulinum* bacteria are dangerous because of the botulinal toxins they produce. Better known as botulism, these toxins are often the cause of lethal cases of food poisoning. In 1978 a tin of Alaskan salmon infected with *Clostridium botulinum* Type E caused the death of two elderly people in Birmingham (UK). A second couple were poisoned by the salmon but survived.[1]

This natural reservoir of death has obvious attractions for the military: biological weapons are both cheap and effective; they offer the sort of choices – to incapacitate or to kill? – so favoured by military scenarios. There are also some unique disadvantages.

This chapter will look at how biological weapons have been

researched and deployed in the past, their social and medical effects, and current US policy.

Sickness unto death: biological weapons to the Second World War

Technological aids for spreading disease may have changed over the centuries. However, biological warfare, in some form or other, has been practised for a long time.

Two thousand years ago the Greeks and Romans used human and animal corpses with great effect to poison wells of drinking water. Similar tactics were employed more recently in the American Civil War and in the Boer War. Less crude, perhaps, was the practice of throwing the bodies of plague victims over the walls of cities under siege. The Tartars employed this strategem against the Genoese in Crimea in 1346. So successful were these attacks that the Genoese were forced to leave. In so doing, they helped spread the Black Death – another name for the plague – to Italy. Four centuries later bodies were used with similar effect against besieged cities in the Russo–Swedish war of 1710.[2]

A more sophisticated strategem for using biological warfare was that employed by the British in their war of attrition against the American Indians. Sir Jeffrey Amherst, the British commander-in-chief in North America, wrote to his subordinate, Colonel Henry Bouquest (then opposing Indians in Ohio and Pennsylvania), 'Could it not be contrived to send the Small Pox among these disaffected tribes of Indians?' Bouquest replied that he would see to the matter. He needn't have bothered. A Captain Ecuyer at Fort Pitt had already handed over some presents. The captain demonstrated his regard for the Indians by giving two hostile chiefs 'two blankets and a handkerchief out of the Small Pox hospital. I hope it will have the desired effect.'[3]

The effect which Ecuyer expected would have occurred some 9–12 days after the chiefs had received their gifts. It would have taken the form of a fever, fatigue, severe backache, headaches and stomach pain. A rash would appear – particularly on the face – and this would develop into pustules. Death usually occurs at this stage in about 30 per cent of cases – as with the Indians – where there has been no vaccination. Those who survived would have seen the pustules heal and form a scab which would peel off to leave a permanent deep scar.[4] During the twentieth century a great deal of research and experiment has gone into perfecting Ecuyer's technique.

British research into biological warfare was initially conducted at the chemical warfare establishment at Porton Down in Wiltshire. Although there had been interest in the subject in official circles since 1934, the first highly secret laboratory was built only in 1940. According to one of its first occupants it was 'a primitive affair – little more than an old wooden army hut'. Seven years later, in recognition of the importance of the subject, the British government built a separate building at Porton to house the Microbiological Research Establishment. Said to be the largest brick building in Britain at the time, the new laboratory was to continue – and expand – the work on biological warfare.[5] According to a recently declassified report prepared for Britain's Joint Chiefs of Staff Committee (during wartime, the prime minister's advisers), and dated 12 November 1945, a weapon for brucellosis was at an 'advanced stage of development'.[6] The report (by an Inter-Services Sub-Committee on Biological Warfare) stated that *Brucella* would be used in a 500lb cluster bomb. Inside this would be 106 special bomblets, each containing infectious spores of the bacterium.

Post-war research was largely a continuation of British policy during the Second World War. The British had been concerned that the Germans might use biological weapons and, consequently, launched an intensive research programme. This programme, according to a statement by the Ministry of Defence in 1946, was purely for defensive purposes.[7] On 22 May 1944 the prime minister, Winston Churchill, sent a personal minute to Lieutenant-General Sir Hastings Ismay, his representative on the Chiefs of Staff Committee. The minute explained Britain's interest in biological weapons. Churchill, noting that great progress had been made in bacteriological warfare, referred to the order for a 'half million [anthrax] bombs from America for use should this mode of warfare be employed against us'.[8] Churchill had been told by his military advisers – and he agreed with them – that the only deterrent for biological weapons, should the

Germans use them, was the ability to retaliate in kind.[9] The US also subscribed to this view.

There were, however, problems with Churchill's order. In 1941 and 1942, scientists from Porton Down had used the island of Gruinard (off the West coast of Scotland) as a testing ground for anthrax bombs. Sheep had been used in the trials to test the theory that anthrax could be spread from an air-bursting bomb. The tests showed that it could. On the basis of this work, and more research at Porton Down, some calculations were made on the quantity of anthrax bombs required to attack cities in Germany. Churchill's order of 500,000 bombs was an optimistic request. Some time later it was shown that, for the effect envisaged, the initial estimates were too low by a factor of 8.5. There was no hope of a larger order being met, however, let alone the original one. Difficulties in the loading of the bombs with anthrax remained a problem until the end of the war and delayed deliveries.[10]

These problems were known to the Chiefs of Staff Committee. On 27 July 1944, the Joint Planning Staff (JPS) – a sub-committee of the Chiefs of Staff – produced a report on chemical and biological weapons. On the use of biological weapons, the JPS thought that a 4lb bomb charged with anthrax and used on a 'large scale from aircraft might have a major effect on the course of the war'. However, the JPS acknowledged that supplies were such that there was 'no likelihood of a sustained attack being possible much before the middle of 1945'.[11]

Events overtook this suggestion. The war in Europe was over by May 1945 and no weapons of mass destruction – such as anthrax bombs – were required to hasten its progress. As far as British war policy during the Second World War was concerned, anthrax bombs were a non-starter.[12]

At the end of 1945, however, the UK Ministry of Defence reviewed the status of CBW. In an appendix to their report on the 'Potentialities of Weapons of War during the Next Ten Years' the Chiefs of Staff's Joint Technical Warfare Committee re-examined the calculations made about the potential of anthrax in 1944.[13] Allowing for a 25 per cent failure rate, it was estimated that 4,277,100 4lb anthrax bombs would kill half the population in the six German cities of Aachen, Wilhemshafen, Stuttgart, Frankfurt, Hamburg and Berlin. The bombs could be delivered from a larger 500lb cluster bomb containing 106 anthrax bomblets. Two thousand six hundred and ninety Lincoln aircraft would be required to drop 40,350 of these cluster bombs.[14]

To assist the Chiefs of Staff in their deliberations the Deputy Director of Special Weapons and Vehicles in the war office, Brigadier Wansbrough-Jones, penned a further minute to his superiors on 3 December 1945.[15] The brigadier extolled the virtues of biological agents, and pointed out that much smaller concentrations of anthrax, or brucellosis bacterium, would be required to injure or kill people than, for example, the nerve gas tabun developed by the Germans during the Second World War. Arguing the case for continued research on biological weapons, Wansbrough-Jones felt that

> Biological warfare need not remain a method of warfare repugnant to the civilised world. The further development of types such as US [brucellosis] coupled with a certain amount of informed guidance of the public might well result in it being regarded as very humane indeed by comparison with atom bombs.

And he added that biological weapons might be used 'in minor wars on which it was not worth using atom bombs; or major ones in which they were being barred'. In a somewhat optimistic vein he speculated that further research might 'lead to such strong defence that ultimately this form of warfare will be valueless, though it may pass through a phase in which offence clearly leads defence.' But if Britain didn't continue this work he feared that other countries might, and the position of the UK would be bad 'if other countries develop an effective weapon'. Regrettably, 40 years on, biological weapons are still being investigated, and offence still leads defence. Besides, the great problem with investigation is that it tends to lead to implementation.

Circumstantial evidence suggests that at least one British scientist actually encouraged the use of biological warfare agents during the Second World War. According to the authors of *A Higher Form of Killing*,[16] Czech partisans were supplied with grenades containing the toxin botulism to use in an assassination attempt on Reinhard Heydrich, the Reichsprotektor of Bohemia and Moravia. Heydrich – Hitler's personal choice as the man to succeed him as Führer – was able to integrate his Protectorate into the German war economy. He was so successful that the Allies agreed to assist in his assassination. In the attack Heydrich was hit by grenade splinters; according to the doctors who examined him, his injuries were not particularly severe. But Heydrich died. The official cause of death was septicemia. British scientists suspect that the grenades used in the ambush contained botulinus toxins. And the scientist Paul Fildes, said to be responsible for supplying the grenades, apparently remarked to a colleague that Heydrich's murder 'was the first notch on my pistol'.

Far more serious, and fully substantiated, is Japanese experimentation with biological weapons during the Second World War. Large areas in China were used as a testing ground. The programme was carried out in great secrecy. Suspicions were aroused at the time because of two unnatural outbreaks of plague in which only humans were affected; no disease was found in animals. Normally, outbreaks in humans follow an epidemic in the rat population. Fleas transmit the disease from rats to humans. The Chinese suspicions were communicated in a note in July 1942 from General Chiang Kai-Shek to Winston Churchill.[17]

More details about Japan's biological warfare programme were revealed at a war crimes tribunal held by the Soviet Union at Khabarovsk in 1949 and given wide coverage in the Soviet media.[18] Because much of the information was provided by Japanese prisoners-of-war, some have questioned its validity. In 1976, however, it became clear that the evidence heard at Khabarovsk was only the tip of the iceberg. A television programme put out by the Tokyo Broadcasting Company carried interviews with 20 of the former members of Japan's biological warfare unit in China. Not only did the interviewees confirm that the experiments were wide-ranging, they also claimed that the US had been told about the extent of this work in 1946. In 1945 Japan had stocks of biological weapons far larger than those of any other nation.

The disturbing feature of these revelations is the fact that it took 27 years to confirm that the testimony of the Khabarovsk prisoners-of-war was correct. Such was the fear of 'Soviet Communism' in the West in 1949 and 1950 that anything that was said in the Soviet Union was clearly categorised as suspect. The Khabarovsk trials were thus effectively dismissed as propaganda. The general public in the West did not learn about the grisly details of the Japanese biological weapons programme until official US government documents were made public.

The documents were released recently under the US Freedom of Information Act and confirm that the US was indeed told about the scale of the Japanese BW programme. Writing in the *Bulletin of Concerned Asian Scholars*, John Powell says that a reading of the documents confirms that the US recognised the value of the Japanese work for its own biological weapons programme.[19] It was decided to do a deal with the Japanese scientists then in US hands; immunity from prosecution was offered in exchange for research programme data. Armed with this information the US decided not to co-operate with the Russians in revealing the extent of this particular area of Japan's wartime atrocities. Convinced that the Japanese had experimented on Soviet prisoners-of-war, the Russians were eager to gather evidence to help convict the Japanese of inhumane practices in wartime.

It now appears that, in the course of testing potential biological weapons, the Japanese scientists experimented on more than 3,000 human guinea pigs. Most of the people so abused were Chinese or Russian prisoners-of-war. Some are said to have been US servicemen – an American survivor testified before a Congressional Committee in June 1982 that US servicemen had been used for some of these experiments.[20] This makes the US decision to do a deal with the Japanese scientists all the more remarkable. All the prisoners were killed in the course of testing biological agents which caused plague, typhus, dysentery, gas gangrene, haemorrhagic fever, typhoid, cholera, tularemia, brucellosis, anthrax and smallpox among others. Most individuals were infected with a disease to see how many would die. In some cases the disease was not allowed to run its course. Curious to study the progress of the infection, the Japanese scientists deliberately killed some prisoners with morphine at various stages of their illness to study the effects of the viruses and bacteria on internal organs.

US eagerness to obtain the results of this work is revealed in a report written by Dr Edward Hill, Chief of Basic Sciences at Camp (now Fort) Detrick in Maryland. With the help of a colleague, Hill interviewed 19 Japanese BW experts and reported his findings to General Alden C. Watt, Chief of the US Chemical Corps. Hill wrote that

> evidence gathered in this investigation has greatly supplemented and amplified previous aspects of this field . . . Information has accrued with respect to human susceptibility to those diseases as indicated by specific infectious doses of bacteria. Such information could not be obtained in our own laboratories because of scruples attached to human experimentation.

Hill went on to say that he hoped 'that individuals who voluntarily contributed this information will be spared embarrassment because of it and that every effort will be taken to prevent this information from falling into other hands.'[21]

The Camp Detrick scientist had no need to worry, for the information remained secret until the Japanese television programme exposed the cover-up. Further Japanese revelations about the activities of Unit 731 which carried out the experiments on prisoners-of-war have been reported.[22] Many of the scientists and doctors who performed the experiments are now directors of Japanese pharmaceutical firms or university professors.[23]

There is no doubt that US failure to co-operate with the Russians and prosecute the Japanese scientists concerned initiated a dangerous level of distrust between the two countries. The distrust surfaced several years later during the Korean war when the US was accused by North Korea and China of conducting biological warfare. Apparently unexplained outbreaks of plague, anthrax, smallpox, cholera and plant disease prompted the accusation.[24] At the invitation of the North Koreans, a tribunal of internationally known scientists was convened to examine the evidence. The tribunal, in a carefully researched report, concluded that the evidence did indeed suggest that the US was guilty of using biological weapons. The US, however, vehemently denied this. Although the Americans suffered some political damage over the tribunal's conclusions the case still remains one which is essentially unproven. It must be said, however, that there was a good deal of circumstantial evidence to support the tribunal's findings.[25]

The doubts and distrust continue. The cost, in terms of human life, will be great.

Candidates for biological warfare – and their effects

As one might suspect, some of the requirements for a biological weapon are fairly obvious. Unlike chemical weapons, only a small quantity of biological agent would be required to start an epidemic. The organisms used live and multiply inside their host, eventually overwhelming the body defences. In selecting an organism to be used, a principal requirement is that it be reasonably robust and able to withstand the processes used to make it into a weapon. Most biological agents have a limited life in storage during which their biological activity is continually declining.[26] To offset having to use much larger quantities of a less active preparation, steps would have to be taken continually to replenish stocks. As a means of slowing down the rate of decay, agents would either be stored at very low temperatures – the lower the better – or else dried in a gentle manner by freeze-drying.

When they come to be used, most biological agents would be dispersed in a form of aerosol. A typical bomblet, designed expressly for spreading a dried preparation of the agent, might have a small cylinder of compressed air arranged to direct an air current up through the powdered agent – or along a surface – and out of an exit port.[27] Biological agents can also be spread by guided missiles; dispersed from aircraft tanks as a powder, or slurry (some are not stable in an aerosol); or even used in cluster bombs. Efficient dispersal of an agent is crucial to its successful use; no less important is the viability of the organism once it has been sprayed.

In the 1950s, Britain and the USA both conducted extensive tests on dispersal. Both countries believed themselves to be vulnerable to attack by biological agents. To test this hypothesis, live bacterial organisms were released in experiments to monitor their movement. British scientists conducted tests with apparently lethal bacteria in the Caribbean and off the western coast of Scotland. The tests, code-named Operations Harness, Cauldron and Hesperus, were first revealed by two British journalists, Robert Harris and Jeremy Paxman, in their book *A Higher Form of Killing*.[28] According to the authors, the details of the British tests are still classified secret.

Tests in the USA were conducted with live, supposedly harmless bacteria. In September 1950 two US Navy minesweepers located off the Californian coast released sufficient bacteria to contaminate 117 square miles of the San Francisco area. In their report of the operation the scientists wrote that nearly every one of the 800,000 inhabitants of the city had inhaled the bacteria. Any other city with similar climatic conditions, they said, would be equally vulnerable to attack. In further tests in the state of Virginia, the subways of New York and the Canadian city of Winnipeg, the scientists proved how vulnerable cities were to attack by biological agents.[29] The British studies are still classified because it is thought that they demonstrate just how vulnerable the UK is to an attack of this kind.

The robustness of an organism is most important when it has been sprayed, for the agent needs to be active for some time after its dispersal in order to cause injury. Temperature, humidity and ultraviolet light can all influence the viability of a biological agent in the field. Suitable candidates for weapons would be chosen with these factors in mind. An organism which was very sensitive to extremes of temperature might therefore only be used in a temperate climate at certain times of year. In similar fashion the other factors affecting viability would be taken into account before the weapon was fired.

All these strictures do not apparently prevent there being a long list of potential biological agents. The candidates which have been considered as potential biological weapons are listed in Table 3 (see p. 115). It is clear that there are agents to suit most circumstances.

For an epidemic, a highly contagious (i.e. transmitted from person to person) virus or bacteria would probably be selected. It would then be necessary to decide two questions. Is a high mortality rate required? Or simply the temporary incapacitation of people in order to allow one's own troops to gain the upper hand? Needless to say, there is a candidate for both eventualities. An influenza virus or pneumonic plague bacillus would satisfy the requirements for a highly contagious agent transmitted by human contact. In the great influenza pandemic of 1918–19, it is estimated that some 20 million people died – and this number represented only 3 per cent of all those who had the illness (in other words, a low mortality rate).[30] With pneumonic plague, the percentage of victims who died would be many times greater.[31]

High on the list of incapacitants is brucellosis. Caused by the *Brucella* species of bacteria, this is an acute, or chronic infection in people and domesticated animals. The disease occurs worldwide. In infected animals (cattle, sheep and pigs), it usually causes them to abort. In people, infection is caused by skin contact – through small abrasions – by eating or drinking infected material (often milk), or by inhaling the organism. The brucellosis bacterium can be produced easily in fermenters (similar in many respects to those used for making beer) and when dried it retains its virulence for years. When moist and in the environment, it will remain active for weeks. The incubation period after exposure varies between two and four weeks. Symptoms are variable, but usually take the form of a severe chill, a recurrent fever, sweating, headache, loss of appetite, extreme exhaustion, aching joints and depression. These last for 2–4 weeks, but could continue for longer. Periodic relapses are common (with a recurrence of the symptoms) and could continue for years.[32]

The bacterium which causes brucellosis has been recognised as a potential incapacitant for some time. In the report prepared for the Joint Chiefs of Staff Committee on 12 November 1945 (see p. 28) a major factor in favour of the organism was that it did not cause epidemics. Any contamination of the ground would be only temporary – days rather than weeks or years – and cities, therefore, would not need to be evacuated. As for the production processes, these were relatively simple. The sub-committee anticipated that the 'effort and time necessary to produce bombs for an effective operation, such as the saturation of 6 major [German] cities may be very much less than is required for anthrax.' *Brucella*, it said, 'produces incapacitation for months' and 'it is not fatal to man, whereas anthrax usually is.' Nevertheless, even though brucellosis lasts for only a few weeks, its effects are likely to persist through recurrence for some time after the fighting has ceased.

As we have seen, anthrax figured as large as brucellosis in wartime research. Why anthrax? There are numerous probable reasons why this was selected. Its lethal nature and ease of manufacture would be just two. Caused by the bacterium *Bacillus anthracis*, anthrax is a disease which affects various domestic animals and people. Human cases are usually caused through contact with infected animals; hair, hide, meat and bones are all sources of infection as employees in abattoirs are all too aware. Transmission between humans is rare, however. Infection occurs by skin contact – through an abrasion, by inhalation or by ingestion. About one-fifth of people who contract the disease through skin contact die. The mortality rate through inhalation is much higher. It is estimated that about 80 per cent of untreated (human and livestock) cases who contracted the disease through inhalation – the 4lb (air-bursting) bombs envisaged by the Joint Planning Staff in 1944 (see p. 29) were designed with this in mind – would die from septicemia.[33] There would also be the problem of contamination. Anthrax spores persist in the environment for decades. Forty years after Porton Down scientists conducted their experiments with anthrax on Gruinard, the island is still contaminated and out of bounds to the public.[34]

Were anthrax used as a weapon today, it would be possible to offer some protection with vaccines. The efficiency of the vaccines in cases of heavy exposure, and particularly through inhalation, is still an area of doubt. For those with the disease, treatment with antibiotics would be essential. A course of treatment would take weeks. As for any food which was contaminated, this would require prolonged sterilisation before it could be considered safe to eat. (Claims that anthrax is under investigation as a biological weapon by the Russians are considered below.)

Biological weapons are *persistent*: anthrax pollutes the environment for years; brucellosis recurs. The latter is one of the major dangers that would be encountered were a virus to be transmitted by an insect carrier. Yellow fever is a case in point. This is a highly dangerous disease. Between the seventeenth and nineteenth centuries it decimated whole populations. Fatalities were still common in the twentieth century when as many as one-third of patients died.[35]

According to a 1960 report from the US Chemical Corps (and not long declassified) yellow fever was considered to have all the makings of 'an extremely effective BW [biological warfare] agent'.[36] The corps began work on it in 1953 at Fort Detrick, the US Army's biological warfare research centre. Yellow fever was chosen because it is transmitted by a mosquito, *Aedes aegypti*, and, as far as the corps was concerned, an insect carrier had great potential in biological warfare. Not only did the mosquito inject the virus directly into the body, rendering any protection offered by a mask ineffective, but the mosquitoes would 'remain alive for some time, keeping an area constantly dangerous'. The mosquitoes, however, are just part of the problem. The real danger occurs when a reservoir of the virus becomes established in an animal population. Although the *Aedes* mosquito prefers to breed in areas of human habitation it can, and does, transfer its virus to animals. To propagate, all viruses need to grow in living tissues. In nature the host is usually an animal – primates are often affected. On the other hand, in the laboratory the host might be a chick embryo or a colony of cells growing in a special culture medium. Once in a host the virus multiplies rapidly and a new reservoir of infection is established. A mosquito which succeeded in consuming blood from this new host would transfer the yellow fever virus to numerous others and help to spread the disease.

Outbreaks of yellow fever in human habitats can now usually be controlled. It is impossible, however, to stop the spread of the disease to animals, and a source of reinfection is always present. This situation is all too common in parts of Africa and Central and South America.

The fact that yellow fever has never occurred in Asia was seen by the US Chemical Corps as a distinct advantage. It was very probable, the corps argued, that the 'population of the USSR would be quite susceptible to the disease'. In the view of the corps, an attack with the *Aedes aegypti* mosquito would be difficult to detect, particularly if this type of mosquito lived in the area. (*Aedes* frequents habitats between latitudes 40°N and 40°S.) Even if an attack were suspected, it could not be confirmed until the disease broke out, two or three days later. Although there is a yellow fever vaccine which is effective in preventing the disease, the corps considered that it 'would be impossible for a nation such as the USSR to quickly undertake a mass-immunization program to protect millions of people'. It was concluded that these difficulties of detection and prevention make yellow fever an effective biological weapon.

In 1959 it seems that arrangements for using yellow fever as a biological weapon were well in hand. Fort Detrick had the capacity to produce 0.5 million mosquitoes a month; a plant capable of producing 130 million insects a month had been designed. The corps proposed the construction of a 'large-scale facility' for producing a mosquito-borne yellow fever virus. This would be disseminated in '2½lb containers of the 750lb cluster [bomb]; 4.5inch spherical bombs for aircraft dispensers; and 3.4inch spherical bombs of the BW SERGEANT warhead [a missile-guided system]'.

The danger of creating a reservoir of disease in animals is not the only problem with biological weapons; they are unpredictable in other ways. For example, there is the danger of mutation. This is a particular problem with viruses which often mutate and develop new strains. In the course of a biological attack with a contagious virus there is a chance that a new, equally virulent strain will develop as the virus passes through the population.[37] There would then be a real possibility that the biological weapon could backfire. The mutant virus strain would infect the troops of the invading army – inoculated against the original virus, but susceptible to the new mutant strain – who in turn would carry the infection home. No one would escape. The perpetrators and victims would all suffer.

Contagious viruses would appear, therefore, to be just too

unpredictable. Indeed, it was for this very reason that the US appears to have rejected this type of agent as a potential biological weapon. Testifying before a Congressional Committee in June 1969, a spokesperson for the US Department of Defense stated: 'we have had a policy that the biological agents that we would try to develop would be noncontagious.' He went on to explain the reasons:

> A contagious disease would not be effective as a biological warfare agent, although it would have devastating effects. It lacks the essential element of control – since there would be no way to predict or control the course of the epidemic that might result.[38]

There are, however, more subtle biological weapons which can be used to kill individuals rather than large numbers of people and which are not the products of bacteria, viruses or the like. These are the toxins. Ricin, a toxic protein in the castor bean, is one. Long recognised as a hazard in the manufacture of castor oil, ricin was developed as a biological weapon in the US during the Second World War. The protein, which is sensitive to heat and easily destroyed, served as a useful model for work being carried out on other biological weapons.[39] US interest in ricin appears to have continued for some time after the war. On 3 July 1952 the US Department of the Army filed a patent for the preparation of toxic ricin.[40] Significantly, the patent was only published 10 years later, when the army was probably no longer concerned about the details of its patent being made public.

The US was not alone in recognising the value of ricin. In their experiments on prisoners-of-war in Unit 731 the Japanese tested ricin by adding it to food. According to the transcripts of the Khabarovsk trial, Senior Sergeant Mitomo Kazuo testified[41] that on some of the prisoners he

> experimented 5–6 times, testing the action of Korean bind-weed, heroin, bactal and castor-oil seeds. One of the prisoners of Russian nationality became so exhausted from the experiments that no more could be performed on him, and Matsui [a senior officer, not on trial] ordered me to kill that Russian by

giving him an injection of potassium cyanide. After the injection that man died.

This horrifying testimony and its revelations may have been news to the interrogators. Perhaps not. Whatever the truth of the matter, it is reported that the Soviet Union also valued the protein from the castor bean. So much so, it seems, that it was used in assassination attempts by Bulgarians on two exiles. One attempt succeeded. Georgi Markov, an exile resident in London, was killed in September 1978 by a pellet containing ricin which had been shot into his leg. The second attempted killing, this time in Paris, was a failure. Vladimir Kostov was hit in the back with a pellet 10 days before Markov was shot. Heavy clothing worn as a protection against the cold slowed the passage of the microscopic pellet and it lodged in the skin on Kostov's back where it could do little harm.[42]

Thus a cool autumnal day prevented another biological weapon from achieving a 100 per cent kill rate. The vagaries of the weather continue to dog the footsteps of biological weapons, and will probably always do so. For the moment, though, it seems that research will continue. As long as it does, it will pose threats and, in the case of use, insuperable difficulties to medical workers.

Medical workers and biological weapons

Fears have been expressed that breweries or laboratories producing antibiotics or vaccines might be converted to biological weapons production. The conversion, it is argued, is a relatively simple process because similar manufacturing procedures are involved. But this is not quite true, as the Stockholm International Peace Research Institute pointed out over 10 years ago.[43] What the processes have in common is a procedure for encouraging the growth of bacteria in a vat which contains suitable nutrients. The procedure can be carried out on a single-batch basis or, by altering the supply of nutrients, changed to a continuous culture from which the organisms are constantly removed. Where the procedures for vaccines and weapons differ, however, is in the safety precautions required in their manufacture. The fermentation process to produce antibiotics or beer does not require stringent safety precautions to prevent contamination of staff or the environment. Fermentation is usually carried out under pressure in order to exclude unwanted micro-organisms from the process. With dangerous pathogens for biological weapons, exactly the opposite is required. Pathogenic bacteria will probably be grown under negative pressure to prevent any organism escaping.

In many ways vaccine production facilities offer more suitable sites than others for biological weapons production. However, the scale of protection afforded staff is still much less than with biological weapons. For vaccines living micro-organisms are used, but these are invariably killed after cultivation. Stringent safety procedures are really only required for handling the live organism. In the case of biological weapons, however, the micro-organisms are live, virulent and therefore dangerous at all stages of manufacture. Safety precautions for staff would have to take account of this. As for the staff required to work in these facilities, they would need to be highly skilled. The possibility that industrial laboratories might be converted for biological weapons production cannot be ignored. However, the most likely site for their production is almost certain to be in an official defence laboratory where all stages in the production and testing of a weapon can be carried out away from public scrutiny.

A more pressing problem for medical workers is what could they do in the case of an attack with biological weapons. In all probability, they could do very little. There are basically two forms of defence against biological attack. One would be to inoculate the population. To do this, however, it would be necessary to know what biological weapon would be used. Biological warfare is designed to catch an adversary unawares; it is therefore most unlikely that its nature could be anticipated. In addition, full immunity would take about 14 days, even with repeated inoculations. As a preventive measure, then, inoculation would not be particularly successful.

The second type of defence would be an early-warning system, capable of detecting a biological weapons attack. Detection systems are available for locating unusual organisms in the air.[44]

Most of the organisms used in biological warfare would be dispersed as an aerosol.[45] To enable the organism to be carried by the wind, most particles would vary in size between 1 and 5 millionths of a metre in diameter. (This size also allows particles to penetrate deep into the lungs.) Should particles of this size be detected, most military authorities would be alerted to the possibility that some organism might have been deliberately released. Problems of identification would then follow.

Most toxins and viruses enter cells in the body and disrupt the metabolism. This disruption usually leads to a change in the composition of various blood components. These — enzymes, antibodies and pigments – can be investigated and the progress of the disease assessed. For example, if someone has been exposed to the virus which causes hepatitis, measuring blood enzymes and the pigment bilirubin can be useful in diagnosing whether the patient is infected. However, these measurements on their own are usually only a guide. To confirm that the patient has an infectious form of hepatitis, caused by a virus and resulting in a debilitating liver disease, requires antibodies which are specific to the disease. In a laboratory test the antibodies would only attach themselves to the viral agent if it were hepatitis; with other viruses this reaction would not occur. In this manner it would be possible to confirm the diagnosis.

This procedure is routinely carried out in many hospital laboratories. The task is made easier because the doctor has often made a preliminary diagnosis of the disease and is seeking confirmation. A request for this to be done is therefore very specific. Where the cause of the disease is unknown, however, the task is infinitely more complex. This would be the position in an attack with a biological warfare agent. As most doctors would be unfamiliar with diseases caused by likely biological warfare agents, misdiagnosis would be common for the first few cases. Hospital or special laboratories which had facilities for identifying bacteria, viruses or fungi would be sent a blood sample and asked to identify the agent. With few leads to go on, laboratories would have to do a large number of tests using antibodies to each potential biological weapon. Assuming that these antibodies were available, a result might be available in a matter of days.

But it could take longer than this: weeks might elapse before definite confirmation.

Parallel with these investigations, the specific make-up of the micro-organism (such as its fat or protein content) might be studied using more sophisticated biochemical techniques in a specialist defence laboratory. The results obtained would be compared with those from known biological warfare agents.

Treatment would, to a large extent, be determined by the organism to which the victim was exposed. If infections are caused by a virus, urgent treatment with very specific antibodies would be required. In general, such antibodies would not be available and, in any case, would not guarantee success. Immunity to a virus can only be obtained if the body builds up its defences in preparation – and this requires prior treatment with killed forms of the virus. Where the type of virus to be used is unknown, this protection can only be guesswork.

For an attack with bacterial agents antibiotics would be required to kill bacteria. It would be necessary to have adequate stocks of broad-spectrum antibiotics – ones that act on a number of organisms – as well as some more specific drugs. For many patients, artificial respiration and other intensive medical supervision would be required.[46] Such measures require hospitalisation. Many patients with infections would probably need to stay in hospital for some 2–3 weeks. Where beds are at a premium – as they are in most hospitals even in developed countries – this would mean that only a proportion of victims, maybe as low as one-third, could be properly treated. Most of the fatalities would occur amongst those people who failed to get hospital treatment. (In chapter 5 some examples are given of the likely casualties in an attack with biological weapons.)

For a short time in the early 1970s, it seemed as though these terrible consequences of biological weapons use had been understood. Present indicators, however, are not so reassuring.

The Biological Weapons Convention and after

In November 1969, President Nixon, in a major policy statement, announced that the US would not be the first to use chemical weapons in a war. Furthermore, he said that the US renounced the use of 'lethal biological agents and weapons' and in future would 'confine its biological research to defensive measures such as immunization and safety measures'. The Department of Defense, Nixon affirmed, had been asked to make 'recommendations as to the disposal of existing stocks of bacteriological weapons'.[47] Nixon's gesture, and the disposal of the stocks of biological agents, gave added impetus to the campaign to outlaw biological warfare, which resulted in the 1972 Biological Weapons Convention.

Announcing the US decision to destroy its BW stockpile, the US delegate stated that it was his government's considered judgement that 'retaliation in kind would not be the best military response to a biological attack'. The reasons given included the unpredictability of biological weapons, their delay in causing an effect, the danger of causing large numbers of civilian casualties and, most important, the fact that these weapons 'could not destroy the military arsenal – the tanks, planes and artillery – of an enemy.'[48]

With the destruction of the US stockpile (July 1971–October 1972) the extent of the American effort on biological weapons became clear. In 1969, a Department of Defense spokesperson indicated that the potential biological weapons under investigation in the US – for both offensive and defensive purposes – had included four incapacitating and six lethal anti-personnel agents (these are all listed in Table 3, p. 115).[49] The list was longer than this, however, and included a fifth incapacitating and two anti-crop agents. Not all of these agents were suitable for weapons. It seems that only eight were stockpiled, and these stocks, according to the Department of Defense, were destroyed in 1971–2.[50] The agents destroyed included two fungi which would cause disease in rice and cereal crops respectively, and six anti-personnel agents, three of which were incapacitants, the other three being lethal micro-organisms. The incapacitating agents destroyed included the bacterium which caused brucellosis. The lethal agents were the virus for yellow fever and the bacteria which caused tularemia and anthrax.

The 1972 Convention represented a significant breakthrough

in military thinking about biological weapons. However, it did nothing about chemical weapons. It merely called on the parties concerned to negotiate in good faith to secure a new treaty outlawing chemical warfare – and we are still awaiting one. Furthermore, the US has since supported accusations that the Soviet Union is stockpiling biological weapons – thus exacerbating international tension and, inevitably, strengthening the case for continued US research in the area.

One of the most sustained of these attacks dates from October 1979 and November 1980 when reports appeared in the Russian-language emigré magazine *Possev* alleging that bacteriological accidents had occurred in the Soviet Union. The second of the two reports referred to an incident at the city of Sverdlovsk where an explosion in a military settlement was said to have resulted in the release of anthrax. In March 1981 this story was given great publicity by the western media. Allegations were made that the Soviet Union was stockpiling biological weapons in violation of international laws. The US State Department announced that it had asked the Soviet Union for an explanation of the incident. The Soviet authorities were quick to respond. According to the official news agency, TASS, there had indeed been an anthrax epidemic in Sverdlovsk.[51] Acknowledging that anthrax had never been completely eradicated from the Urals, TASS said the latest incident had been caused by adverse weather conditions which had made sheep and cattle susceptible to contagious diseases. Lack of personal hygiene in tending livestock, and the purchase of unbranded meat, wool, and hides from unauthorised individuals, had exacerbated the problem.

This explanation did not satisfy the US, however, which claimed some days later that it had evidence to refute the Soviet version of the anthrax incident.[52] The US is still unconvinced. In his annual report to Congress, Defense Secretary Caspar Weinberger claimed, on 8 February 1982, that the US had 'evidence of an inadvertent release of anthrax bacteria from a highly secured military installation in the Soviet city of Sverdlovsk during the Spring of 1979'.[53] He went on to claim that the evidence 'points strongly, we believe, to biological warfare preparations in the Soviet Union that exceed those allowed under the treaty for protective purposes.'

One view of events suggests that the US Defense Secretary is wrong to dismiss the Soviet answer so lightly. According to Zhores Medvedev – an internationally renowned Russian biochemist, now resident in London – an analysis of the incident suggests that it could have been caused by infected livestock, or by an accident in a laboratory where an anthrax vaccine is produced. Medvedev argues that, as anthrax is still a problem in parts of the Soviet Union, it is almost certain that research and development work is carried out on anthrax vaccines. This work is likely to be done in research centres not frequented by the public because the anthrax vaccine has to be made from live, and still virulent, bacteria. As vaccination only confers immunity for about a year, revaccination is essential. And the vaccine itself is only viable for two years. If sufficient stocks are to be maintained, large-scale cultivation of anthrax bacterium and the production of anthrax spores has to be a continuous operation.

More doubt is cast on the US version of events by the fact that an American scientist was visiting Sverdlovsk at the time of the alleged anthrax epidemic. In an interview reported in the *New York Times* (25 November 1981), Donald Ellis, Professor of Physics and Chemistry at Chicago's Northern Western University, claimed that he moved about the city unhindered, even leaving and returning to Sverdlovsk on one occasion. Such movement would have been forbidden in the event of a real accident, which probably explains why Ellis noted nothing untoward during his stay.

Unfortunately, without an independent investigation of the incident, neither the Soviet nor the US version of the events can be substantiated. In view of this stalemate, the Sverdlovsk accident will be added to the growing inventory of alleged biological and chemical warfare incidents. The list is considerable. Most of the incidents are unproven because, as in the Sverdlovsk case, open inspection of the locations where the incidents were said to have occurred has not been possible.

The way in which the incident was taken up in the West points in one direction: it is clear that the US still envisages biological warfare as a distinct possibility in spite of the 1972 Convention. Initial rumours that the US Army had a budget of 'hundreds of millions of dollars'[54] to spend on biological weapons have been denied by the army. Any suggestion that the army may have been interested in using the revolutionary techniques of genetic engineering to develop more efficient incapacitating biological weapons is not correct, the army says.[55] However, in a statement of July 1982 the army claimed that it had a medical research budget of $17 million for the development of vaccines and ways of treating natural diseases or those caused by potential biological warfare agents. Detectors for identifying biological weapon agents are also under investigation, in particular sensitive instruments which use chemical luminescence to detect bacteria and viruses. Finally the 'intelligence community' has a small budget of $200,000 to monitor any developments in biological warfare which might make the US and NATO forces vulnerable to an attack with biological agents.[56]

Of course, everyone must hope that the Convention does discourage work on biological warfare for, with the new technique of genetic engineering, many and more varied biological agents are possible. It would be feasible to use genetic engineering to produce many more strains of viruses. Bacteria could be produced which were resistant to most antibiotics in common use. Novel plant pathogens which could wipe out whole regions of cultivated crops could also be developed using genetic engineering.[57] The possibilities are endless, as we shall see in chapter 8.

4. Yellow rain

If the US is to be believed, powerful biological warfare agents made with fungal toxins are being used in Indo-China and Central Asia.[1] According to the US State Department, government forces in Laos, Kampuchea and Afghanistan are using weapons made with fungal toxins (mycotoxins) to kill dissident tribespeople and enemy soldiers. The weapons are being supplied by the Soviet Union and have killed thousands of people.

These charges have been denied by the Soviet government as well as by the other governments accused. They all claim that the allegations have been fabricated as a ploy on the part of the US to justify its own declared programme to produce novel binary chemical weapons.[2]

The first major public pronouncement on the subject was made by former US Secretary of State Alexander Haig, in a speech in Berlin on 13 September 1981. Secretary Haig considered his timing. With public opposition to the US nuclear defence programme increasing daily in Europe, and several European governments beginning to have doubts about cruise missiles being deployed in NATO countries, the US needed something to strengthen the resolve of its allies. The US was also anxious to reassure NATO partners that it was not indulging in unnecessary sabre-rattling. The accusation that the Soviet Union not only had an interest in, but was actually using, chemical and biological warfare was ideally suited to bolster morale and reassure the doubters.

Announcing the State Department findings, Secretary Haig – aiming his message over the heads of some 30–80,000 West Berliners demonstrating against US policy and his visit to Germany – claimed that the US had 'obtained good evidence that rather than a traditional lethal chemical agent, three potent mycotoxins' had been used.[3] The evidence to which he referred was found in the course of the

> analysis of a leaf and stem sample from Kampuchea [which] has revealed high levels of mycotoxins of the trichothecene group. The levels detected were up to twenty times greater than any recorded natural outbreak. Since normal background levels of these toxins are essentially undetectable, the high levels found are considered to be abnormal, and it is highly unlikely that such levels could have occurred in a natural intoxication. In point of fact these mycotoxins do not occur naturally in South-East Asia.[4]

Secretary Haig's message had the desired effect. The horrific accounts of the effects of the mycotoxin weapons on villagers were given extensive coverage by press, radio and television and it has remained a subject which is calculated to outrage.

Subsequently, the State Department has said that mycotoxins on their own, or crude preparations of the fungus which produces them, are being used. The use of mycotoxins – essentially toxic chemicals in the fungi – would violate the 1925 Geneva Protocol; the use of crude preparations of the fungi as weapons would clearly violate the 1972 Biological Weapons Convention.

In spite of the evidence produced in Secretary Haig's September speech in Berlin, many scientists have remained sceptical about the State Department's claim. It was questioned whether conclusive results could be obtained from analysis of a single leaf and stem sample, without other background results to eliminate natural levels of these mycotoxins. The State Department's first document had clearly failed to convince the scientific community.

The State Department's findings, together with some evidence containing reports of spraying incidents in which mycotoxins were dispersed as a yellow spray ('yellow rain' is the term now used to describe the spray) were handed over to a group of UN experts investigating allegations of the use of the chemical weapons. Reports of incidents in which chemicals were being used against Laotians and Kampuchean villagers became more numerous between 1979 and 1981.[5] One report in particular referred to claims that chemical attacks on Meo tribespeople in Laos had resulted in the deaths of over 2,000 people.[6] It was these accounts together with a request from some member governments that led to the formation of the UN expert group. Led by Major General Dr Esmat Ezz, the Director of Scientific Research for the Egyptian Armed Forces, the group was responsible for investigating any allegation of chemical or biological warfare.

In November 1981 the UN group delivered an inconclusive report. It had been refused permission to visit any of the countries where chemical warfare agents were alleged to have been used. The only subjects of reputed chemical attacks available for interview were refugees who had fled to Thailand. According to General Ezz's team, 'all the cases interviewed related alleged chemical attacks which occurred several months earlier, and consequently, the group was unable to detect signs and symptoms which would be suggestive of exposure to chemical warfare agents.'[7]

In 1982, and during the first few months of 1983, a great deal was published on the subject of yellow rain. The sheer volume of information is too great to quote here at length. For the purposes of this book, it is more important to assess what evidence there is, and to examine it critically.

The two major publications on the mycotoxin weapons were issued by the US State Department in March and November 1982.[8] The 32-page report issued in March was apparently a summary of a much longer 500-page special document ('National Intelligence Estimate') completed on 22 December 1981.[9] This larger report was sent to all US government agencies and to the White House to be vetted before being released. Any information which might have allowed others to guess where the US government had obtained its information was excised and the report slimmed down to its final 32-page version.

The March 1982 State Department document refers to 261 separate attacks in Laos in which 6,504 deaths are alleged to have occurred; and to 124 separate attacks in Kampuchea causing the deaths of some '981 persons'. The numbers of incidents and deaths are very specific. By not quoting the names of its sources the US casts doubt on its own report, for it proves impossible to verify. The scientific community remained sceptical of the State Department claims.[10]

Three months later, in June 1982, a Canadian toxicologist – Dr Bruno Schiefer of the University of Saskatchewan – produced a report on yellow rain following a visit to Thailand.[11] In his report – which was submitted to the UN – Schiefer concluded that it appeared 'highly unlikely that the essentials of all the reports [of yellow rain] are products of imagination, fabrication or propaganda'. In one series of interviews, Schiefer talked to several Khmer Rouge soldiers in a camp on the Thai–Kampuchean border. All claimed to have been victims of a chemical attack six days earlier. Their symptoms, Schiefer said, could not have been caused by mycotoxins. He considered tear gas to have been a more likely cause. Of the symptoms described, haemorrhaging at the nose was the most common. Many of the other symptoms reported – nausea, vomiting, lack of muscle co-ordination, fever, diarrhoea – have occurred in other circumstances: the victims of the defoliants sprayed by the US in Vietnam also reported similar symptoms.[12]

Mycotoxins have been responsible for accidental deaths. After 1945, food shortages forced many people in rural areas of the Soviet Union to eat grain which had overwintered in the fields. The grain was mouldy, and many thousands of those eating it consumed considerable quantities of mycotoxins and died. Caught unawares by these deaths, Soviet scientists have since devoted a considerable research effort to the study of mycotoxins. It is a legitimate public health issue. For those concerned with animal husbandry, mycotoxins are also a problem; livestock will generally refuse to eat grain contaminated with the fungi which produce these toxins.

The report issued by the US State Department in November 1982 again alleged use of mycotoxins and provided the results of analyses on blood and urine samples obtained from 'victims'.[13] Mycotoxins were found in these. The toxins were also found in leaf, twig, soil and water samples taken from allegedly sprayed areas. Thus the State Department believed it had now amassed considerable evidence to support its case.

The State Department's euphoria was not to last long. In March 1983 new evidence was released from Australia which has fuelled speculation that yellow rain may not have been introduced to the region deliberately but that it could be of natural origin.[14] Samples of leaves and pebbles said to have been contaminated by yellow rain near the Northern Thailand border town of Ma Fuang have only trace levels of mycotoxins, according to Australian government scientists. They add that mycotoxin levels are so low that they can have no military value.[15]

Pollen grains, which occur naturally in the local rain forests, are a significant constituent of yellow rain samples recently analysed by scientists in the USA, UK and Thailand.[16] US Department officials have suggested that the Russians are using pollen deliberately as a vehicle for transmitting the mycotoxins or the fungus. According to Gary Crocker of the State Department, 'It's not wind-blown pollen, it's commercially collected pollen.' Crocker is reported as saying that the Smithsonian Institution in Washington identified the pollen as daisy, chrysanthemum, and several other species.[17]

Dr Joan Nowicke of the Smithsonian's Natural History Museum denies this. According to the report in the scientific journal *Nature*, Dr Nowicke was consulted by scientists from the US Army's Chemical Systems Laboratory (which has done most of the yellow rain analyses for the State Department). In fact, Dr Nowicke did not do analyses for them. Three people from the US Army attended a 'one-day crash-course in pollen analysis' and then phoned her several times for advice. Dr Nowicke, however, says that it is not possible to identify commercially collected pollen, since widely varying species have similar pollen which is difficult, if not impossible, to distinguish.

An alternative explanation to the State Department's theory could be that the pollen carries mycotoxins of its own accord and that this is a natural phenomenon. *Fusarium semitectum*, one of the species of fungi identified by the Thai scientists in yellow rain material, is transmitted naturally in this way. A joint report made in 1928 by an American and a German pathologist, discusses this problem in relation to disease in banana plantations.[18] The two pathologists recognised that disease-producing fungi could be carried on pollen grains from infected banana plants to healthy ones. Fungi and mycotoxins could be transmitted in similar ways in Laos, Kampuchea and Thailand.

There is also the possibility that bees could be responsible for the transmission of mycotoxin-contaminated pollen, according to reports from a conference held in Boston in April 1983. Bees eat pollen and excrete that which is not digested. At certain times of the year, bees apparently excrete large amounts of pollen. Analysis of some of the 'yellow rain' spots from South-East Asia has revealed that there are several sources of pollen in a single spot (as many as 10 different types of pollen have been identified in some, according to one chemical warfare expert). A bee usually only harvests pollen from a single species of plant – other bees in a hive will feed on a single, but perhaps different, plant. Thus, Dr Nowicke says that it would be hard to imagine that the pollen in the yellow spots was the excreta from a single bee, for the diversity of plant species involved was so great.[19] It is a fact, however, that mycotoxins have only been identified in samples from South-East Asia collected in the dry season, in March and April. None have been found in material collected at other times of the year. Why should this be so? Is this more evidence to support a theory of natural occurrence for the mycotoxins and is it consistent with the behaviour of bees? Or is it simply because those collecting evidence have only been active in the dry period? Nobody has yet been able to answer these questions.

It is a well-known feature of chemical warfare agents that if poisoning is to occur through inhalation, the particles of poison need to be of a size less than 10 microns across (millionths of a metre). Particles of this size will penetrate deep into the lungs. Gary Crocker at the State Department suggests that pollen grains of this size could be selected to poison people with myco-toxins, and these could be delivered by aerial spraying, the alleged means of delivering yellow rain in Laos.[20] Perhaps.

However, there is the fundamental problem of gravity to contend with in this argument, as aerial crop sprayers will attest. To deliver herbicides or pesticides efficiently from the air, the particles have to be *at least* 200 microns across. Particles of 10 microns (1,000 times smaller in volume) have as much chance of settling in Australia as they have in Laos. They will be carried where the wind takes them. In addition there are glaring differences in the reported heights of the aircraft involved in spraying; some say 'tree-top' height, others 5,000 feet – at which spraying would be clearly ineffective. Much of the debate about yellow rain as a chemical weapon hinges on the claims advanced by the State Department that the fungi which produce the mycotoxins do not occur naturally, and that no single fungus could produce the range of mycotoxins which have been identified in samples analysed in US laboratories.

Neither claim is, in fact, correct. The fungi which produce the mycotoxins identified in yellow rain samples are from the genus *Fusarium*. Many species of *Fusarium* – including those which produce the yellow rain mycotoxins – do occur naturally throughout Indo-China. A French mycologist, Francis Bugnicourt, documented their presence in 1939.[21] Soviet scientists also claim that a Vietnamese scientist has documented the presence of *Fusarium* fungi in the south of Vietnam.[22]

The suggestion that no single species of fungus will produce several mycotoxins is contained in the report which Secretary of State George Shultz sent to Congress in November 1982. This is not the experience of Japanese scientists, however. Dr Y.Ueno and five colleagues reported in 1973 that the two fungi *Fusarium tricinctum* and *Fusarium roseum* both produce the toxins T-2 and DAS and others besides (see Table 4, p. 122).[23] As *Fusarium roseum* occurs in Indo-China, this is another reason for suggesting that the toxins may be of natural origin.

Artillery is said to be the principal way of delivering yellow rain in Kampuchea, and thousands are said to have fallen victim. However, despite wide interest in the issue, in the four years that yellow rain is claimed to have been used no bomb, shell or grenade has yet been produced to substantiate that weapons exist for this toxin. The absence of this 'hardware' is of concern to both the Khmer Seri and Khmer Rouge forces fighting in Kampuchea. Both armies would like a weapon to prove their charge that chemical weapons are being used against them. So would the State Department.

Any refutation of the yellow rain allegations has to take

account of the numerous reports of Laotian and Kampuchean refugees who claim to have been sprayed. Many refugees have made these claims and they have told US and other investigators that thousands have died agonising deaths as a result of their contact with the toxins. Their accounts of people vomiting profusely, bleeding internally, bleeding from the mouth and having convulsions before death make grim reading.

The position of the refugees is an extremely complicated one, as one of us found on a visit to Thailand. Most of the claims about the use of yellow rain in Laos are from the Hmong hill tribespeople of northern Laos. Recent interviews with the Hmong people about the yellow rain allegations have been conducted by an Australian social scientist, Grant Evans, of La Trobe University in Australia. His accounts of the interviews – conducted both in Laos and at the Ban Vinai refugee camp in Thailand – were published in 1983.[24]

Evans found it extremely difficult to find refugees at Ban Vinai camp who did not give the impression of having been tutored beforehand in their answers about yellow rain. He also believes that, because of the relative unsophistication of the Hmong people, any deaths from malaria or haemorrhagic dengue fever – both of which occur as local health problems – may be attributed to the chance passing of a MIG aircraft. Many refugees have never seen a direct-spraying incident with yellow rain. Most accounts appear to be anecdotal.

The UN investigative team under General Ezz encountered similar problems when it interviewed refugees about the yellow rain allegations in 1982. In its second report to the UN Secretary General in December 1982, General Ezz's team said that the information it was given differed from that obtained by physicians (who provided information for the State Department) at Ban Vinai camp. Several discrepancies are cited by the UN team. According to the physicians' report, one alleged victim of yellow rain claimed that the substance had killed 80 people, whereas the same victim told the UN team that only one woman died. In another case, the UN team was told that one victim had been ill for 20 days whereas the physicians said it was only 20 minutes.

At the UN team's request, Thai dermatologists Dr Renoo

Kotrajoras and Dr Somnuk Vibulsek examined two Hmong refugees who had skin rashes which they attributed to exposure to chemical agents inside Laos two weeks previously (mycotoxins do cause skin necrosis). Both physicians stated categorically that the skin condition was due to a fungal infection, but that the rash must have been present for at least three months. Blood taken from these two refugees was found to be free of mycotoxins. Similarly, other leaf, twig and soil samples given to the UN team, and said to have been contaminated with yellow rain, also proved to have no mycotoxins on analysis.

The UN team, for a second year running, felt that it had insufficient evidence to either prove or disprove the allegations that chemical warfare agents were being used in Indo-China. Again, the team had not been able to visit Laos or Kampuchea to do an investigation.

It is unfortunate that the UN team was unable to gain access to these countries. Several European countries and the US have questioned this refusal to allow access, and query whether the Laotians or Kampucheans do in fact have something to hide. There are indications that some scientific investigators may be given access to Laos in the not too distant future. The question about UN access to Laos remains unresolved. As for access to Kampuchea, the UN team cannot request this as the UN does not recognise the government in Pnomh Penh.

Although the State Department claims to have detected mycotoxins on a gas mask allegedly used by Soviet troops in Afghanistan, others have not been able to find these toxins on material reputed to be contaminated by yellow rain. The UN experts analysed samples of wheat grains, weapons, a parachute and gas mask supplied by guerillas fighting in Afganistan; no chemical weapons agents were detected on any of them.[25]

The Soviet scientist Professor Nicolai Antonov is the chief scientific expert of the Ministry of Health in Moscow, with responsibility for preventing the exposure of industrial workers and civilians to harmful chemicals. He stated that he did not doubt the work of US scientists, such as Dr Chester Mirocha of the University of Minnesota, when they reported finding mycotoxins in samples allegedly containing yellow rain.[26] Professor

Antonov believes the scientists are reporting their findings accurately. Nevertheless, he is doubtful about the source of the samples and whether or not they have been tampered with. The fact that the UN team was unable to observe mycotoxins in samples of alleged yellow rain material strengthened Professor Antonov's belief that the material was suspect. Australian scientists have also failed to find mycotoxins in leaf and soil samples handed over by Laotian refugees.[27] In their report the Australian government scientists concluded that the yellow spots (allegedly yellow rain) were 'faked and deliberately applied by a brush or spraying device'.[28] The Australian report was prepared by Dr Hugh Crone at the Materials Research Laboratory of the Department of Defence. According to Mr Bill Hayden, the new Foreign Minister, Dr Crone's report had been withheld until after the election which brought the Labor Party to power. The results of the report represent a setback for the State Department's case.

A curious twist to the yellow rain story happened on 7 April 1982 when a US group – Covert Action, which monitors the activities of the intelligence agencies – published a press release claiming that a former CIA employee had been contracted to assassinate two fellow-US servicemen who had been planting false evidence of the use of 'yellow rain'.[29] The employee, Scott Barnes, said that in October and November 1981 he and five others, travelling with false documentation issued by the CIA, were sent to Laos from Thailand to locate and rescue two Americans held as prisoners by the Laotians. When rescue proved impossible, orders were given to kill the two prisoners, whom Barnes believes were not prisoners from the Vietnam war, but persons captured recently. Apparently the team refused the assassination order and disbanded.

Barnes's motive for telling his story was evidently to set the record straight. He alleged that the former CIA officer (and Green Beret) Bo Gritz, who had organised the mission into Laos, claimed that the exercise was merely to rescue US servicemen missing in action. This, said Barnes, was quite untrue. Although Barnes gave his story to ABC–TV news in the US, and to reporters on the *Boston Globe* and *Washington Post*, none of this information was made public. *Pravda*, in Moscow, reprinted the story in detail following Covert Action's press release.

One reason why the US news media did nothing with the story was perhaps because Bo Gritz described Barnes as unreliable and given to fantasy. Gritz, it appears, was assumed to be a more credible witness than Barnes.[30] Yet Barnes, it seems, passed a lie detector test administered by one of America's most experienced polygraphers. Among the questions asked were 'Did you go into Laos?' and 'Were you ordered to assassinate American prisoners of war?'

Barnes's story is almost impossible to prove. It merely exists as a somewhat worrying sideline in the whole yellow rain debate. As for Bo Gritz, he apparently is still infiltrating into Laos. In March 1983 Colonel Gritz surrendered himself to Thai police who charged him with possession of a long-distance radio transmitter/receiver. The offence carries a five-year prison sentence. Gritz said the instrument was to help him locate American prisoners-of-war.[31]

The one outstanding question about the mycotoxins which are said to constitute yellow rain is whether they would, in fact, make a good weapon. Professor Antonov says absolutely not. The most toxic of all mycotoxins said to have been used are 100–1,000 times less toxic than nerve gases. Militarily, it would make no sense to use such an ineffective weapon.[32]

Dr Sharon Watson of the US Army Surgeon General office claims that experiments carried out at Fort Detrick showed that only 35mg of some of these toxins are sufficient to kill a 70kg man.[33] Lower doses, she states, could cause haemorrhaging, one of the symptoms reported by refugees. Dr Watson's figures, however, have not been made public and it is difficult, therefore, to assess her evidence.

There are some who might question the toxicity figures Dr Watson has referred to. Professor Matthew Meselson of Harvard University, a long-standing critic of the US chemical weapons programme, says that if the published evidence from animal studies is to be believed – and it is extensive – then the trichothecenes are not particularly toxic. Meselson also uses the example of a 70kg man to make his point. 'If you strip him naked,' says Meselson, 'and lay him on the ground and assume that he absorbs 10 per cent of everything that falls on his skin – and that is making a large assumption – then it would need 10 kilograms of yellow rain to kill him.' Meselson felt it would be better making the yellow rain into bricks. 'In fact,' he added, 'it would be better to drop rocks on his head.'[34]

A question which is still unanswered, however, is whether or not the levels of mycotoxins found in the blood of certain individuals might not have occurred through a natural intoxication – perhaps by the consumption of contaminated food. The State Department published results of analyses of samples taken from Kampuchea in 1982. Three trichothecene mycotoxins were identified in these in the following concentrations: 109ppm nivalenol, 59.1ppm deoxynivalenol and 3.51ppm of T-2 toxin (ppm = parts per million). A control sample had none of the trichothecenes.[35] The State Department insists that this is proof that the mycotoxins are being applied deliberately, and that these levels are too high to be the result of a natural occurrence. This, however, is not quite correct. Levels of trichothecene mycotoxins of the order of 200–300ppm are said to occur naturally in some plant species in Brazil.[36] High levels of naturally occurring mycotoxins have also been reported from other countries.[37]

The integrity of the leaf and soil samples collected from Laos, Kampuchea and Afghanistan is very much in doubt. Little information is available about how representative the samples might be, and where control samples were collected. In view of this, the US State Department is now providing Laotian and Kampuchean exiles with kits specially designed for the collection of material. People will be encouraged to infiltrate back into the country to collect evidence. Perhaps, then, some more reliable material will come to light for analysis. This is possible but doubts will always remain until samples can be collected in such a way as to rule out any interference.

State Department samples have so far been largely supplied by Dr Amos Townsend, retired former US Air Force colonel and medical officer. He is presently a State Department-funded employee working for the Bangkok-based International Rescue Committee, an organisation involved with refugees in Thailand.

Townsend says yellow rain has been used since 1976 but refuses to provide the information which led him to this conclusion. Concerning those who doubt the existence of yellow rain he will only say: 'Scepticism is valuable, but scepticism with an unwillingness to investigate is worrying.'[38] Few would disagree with this sentiment. The yellow rain allegations demand such an investigation. The evidence available to date on this subject is most confusing and far from convincing. Yellow rain would not appear to be a particularly efficient chemical weapon and the alleged motive for its use is indeed questionable. Only an on-the-ground inspection will finally solve the yellow rain riddle.

Until such time, we will not know whether yellow rain is a natural phenomenon or whether mycotoxins or some other chemical agents such as tear gas are being used in Indo-China and Afghanistan. For the present, a healthy scepticism is the only attitude to adopt.

5. Chemical and biological warfare: military scenarios

History would suggest that chemical and biological weapons are inevitably instruments of mass destruction. But this need not be the case, as advocates of CBW are only too ready to point out. There are weapons for all eventualities, designed for immediate tactical advantage on the battlefield or for longer-term strategic gains.

In the First World War, the use of chemicals by both sides was, in the main, for tactical purposes. For the strategic use of chemical weapons we need only look at the Sino–Japanese and Vietnam wars. In both of these, chemical weapons were used by the technologically more advanced nation. It was the United States which defoliated Vietnam – for tactical and strategic gain – and Imperial Japan which used chemical warfare against poorly-equipped Chinese soldiers.

Essentially, CBW could be described as 'search and denial' weapons. They can be employed to harass an enemy which is widely dispersed or to attack some fortified position. Buildings – unless provided with some air-filtration system – offer little protection. The concentration of chemicals will certainly rise more slowly in a building but, in the absence of any ventilation, it will also fall just as slowly.

The weapons are strictly anti-personnel. In any attack with chemical weapons important strategic targets such as communication posts, power stations, air and seaports and the like will remain intact. Some areas may be put out of action temporarily, however, if sprayed with a persistent nerve gas such as VX. This would be done deliberately to contaminate an area and prevent the enemy using it.[1]

Most attacks with CBW, whether on a small or a grand scale, will usually be clandestine, or surprise operations. In this kind of warfare the element of surprise is all-important. The 'first user' is the one who stands to gain most. Any advantage relies on the enemy being caught unawares and without protective equipment. In these circumstances casualties will be considerable.

The situation would be quite different if an attack were launched against troops who were adequately protected. Casualties, in this situation, would be minimal. In fact, the use of chemical weapons against well-protected troops would almost certainly be counter-productive. An attacker, because of protective equipment, would find manoeuvrability restricted and therefore would be at a distinct disadvantage. This could have fatal consequences on a battlefield where the defenders – protected by their own equipment from chemicals and at full strength – could counter-attack with little difficulty.

On the battlefield itself there are certain operational difficulties with chemical weapons. Troops using them require special training and considerable safety precautions are necessary. Good field intelligence is vital. These tasks would hardly be a serious problem if chemical and biological weapons were predictable, but they are not. There is always a risk that these agents may get out of control. A shift in wind direction could be disastrous and it may be difficult to confine the weapons to a single area for any length of time.

Temperature fluctuation also affects the calculation; the lower the temperature, the slower the rate of gas evaporation. The 1966 field manual for US troops adds another important meteorological condition – that of atmospheric stability.[2] However, according to some advocates of chemical warfare, none of these conditions needs to be taken too seriously. In 1979, before she became Deputy Assistant Secretary for the US Army, Amoretta Hoeber claimed that high winds were the only major concern; other conditions, she felt, could be accounted for and the appropriate chemical chosen to meet the needs of any given situation.[3]

It is clear, Amoretta Hoeber's reassurances apart, that there are several issues which complicate forward planning. Any decision to use CBW would only be arrived at after weighing up all the pros and cons, including the political and diplomatic repercussions which would follow the use of weapons calculated to outrage world opinion.

Assuming that a decision were made to use this method of warfare, when might it be used? What is the strategic value of CBW? This would seem to be considerable. It can be used covertly for subversion and economic warfare. The insidious effects of CBW and particularly biological weapons make them ideally suited for sabotage. Any attack would only be discovered long after the saboteurs had escaped. And the close resemblance between naturally and unnaturally occurring epidemics could easily divert suspicion away from the real cause. Recurrent acts of terrorism and assassination, successive crop failures, unexplained outbreaks of disease and poisoning would certainly create alarm and despondency in any country and could even put the survival of governments at stake. Any country which is reliant on a few species of agricultural crop for both internal consumption and export would be particularly vulnerable to sabotage of this kind.[4]

As far as the use of anti-plant chemicals is concerned one need look no further than Vietnam. During the Vietnam war US forces sprayed an estimated 19 million gallons of herbicides over large tracts of land in Vietnam and Laos. Forests were sprayed with the herbicide Agent Orange as a means of denuding trees of their leafy canopy, with the aim of depriving National Liberation Front soldiers of any protective cover. But it was not just soldiers who were affected. Aware that the mere act of spraying would force people to move, the US Air Force aimed to use herbicides as a sort of population-control measure over large tracts of countryside. As an added inducement to encourage villagers to move, the US also destroyed food crops. The herbicide Agent Blue was used for this purpose – and, according to the distinguished Harvard nutritionist and one-time presidential adviser Professor Jean Meyer, by 1967 anti-crop chemicals had been sprayed over 150,000 acres of cropland.[5] Despite the official US government claim that the shortage of crops would hurt only National Liberation Front soldiers, Meyer argued that the policy of forced starvation would, and did, hurt only those who were vulnerable – the young, the old, and the infirm. When the spraying programme was stopped in 1970 following public criticism, some 600,000 hectares of farmland had been destroyed. This area would have produced about 756,000 tonnes of rice.[6]

So much for the longer-term advantages of chemical weapons. What about the more immediate situation? As a prelude to an attack it might be advantageous to put military installations out of action. Communication centres and command posts, for instance, could be targets for anti-personnel biological weapons which would be inactive by the time an attack occurred. Chemical weapons might serve the same purpose. Amoretta Hoeber has argued that the Soviet Union could well use nerve gases to put NATO nuclear bases out of action before an attack by Warsaw Pact Forces.[7]

On the battlefield itself, one of the main attractions of CBW is the support they give to conventional firepower. Military opinion in this respect has differed. During the Second World War Britain's Joint Chiefs of Staff – the prime minister's military advisers – said that gas should be used only as a supplementary weapon. On the other hand, the US and German military authorities argued that chemical weapons could be decisive on their own if used in sufficient quantities at the right time.[8] Today, the British view of 40 years ago is the orthodox opinion of what would happen in a war between developed nations. In developing countries, however, gas on its own might well be decisive against an ill-equipped guerilla adversary.

Quick-acting anti-personnel chemical weapons are effective over a large area and would be used to flush out well-entrenched troops. The chemicals would cause a large number of casualties particularly if used with other conventional weapons. Used in this way, each would increase the effectiveness of the other. The wide range of weapons and chemicals available makes defence difficult. And if more than one agent were used, as is likely, the defence requirements would be considerable. Modern flame-producing and air-burst high explosive weapons might be used along with nerve gas against troops who were not in a dug-in position. For those who are entrenched, the conventional weapons might be fuel-air explosives. Used against unprepared troops chemical weapons will cause at least as many casualties as conventional weapons.[9] Troops encumbered by protective clothing would be more vulnerable, however, to a conventional attack than to one with chemicals.

In attacks against small enemy positions where high casualty rates were permissible nerve gases could be used to advantage. For greatest effect the gases would be used in surprise attacks of high intensity and short duration, with the objective of giving the enemy little opportunity to don protective clothing.

The British employed this tactic in the First World War with the Stokes Mortar.[10] Designed to fire four-inch mortar bombs – each containing 2 litres of gas – a well-trained team could launch 15 before the first had landed 1,000 yards away. Today the same function would be performed by multiple rocket launchers, missiles (Lance, Pershing and cruise) and cluster bombs dropped by ground support aircraft. In an attack, non-persistent agents would be used to cover the depth of the battlefield, and sufficiently far ahead of troops not to impede advance. Persistent chemicals would be avoided as they would hinder operations. Protective clothing would still have to be worn in case the gases remained longer than planned.

Persistent agents have their uses too. In offensive operations, for example, they might be used to contaminate areas not required immediately, but which would also be denied to the enemy. Mustard gas was deployed for this purpose by the Germans in the fields of France and Flanders in 1917. Persistent agents could also be used to hamper an army's line of retreat. This was the Japanese stratagem against the retreating Chinese army at Ichang in 1941. Another use for these agents might be to afford protection to a rapidly advancing army. In the Ethiopian campaign in 1936 the Italians protected the flanks of their rapidly advancing columns by this method.[11]

For defensive operations, both rapidly clearing and long-lasting nerve gases have a role. A gas which clears rapidly might be used against areas where an enemy is concentrating for attack, whereas a persistent agent might impede advance and perhaps even channel enemy troops onto ground which was at once less favourable for attack but easier to defend. Chemical mines interspersed with ones containing high explosive have been considered in this regard. They have the advantage that they would make mine-clearing operations extremely difficult and hazardous and might well persuade an enemy to look for alternative approaches.[12]

As the enemy approached, chemical weapons could be used to harass – forcing soldiers to don masks, causing discomfort and slowing their advance. In the First World War chemical artillery was used for this purpose. The chemicals used in this way need not be lethal – incapacitating agents such as CS would do just as well, as the US discovered in Vietnam. CS gas was often pumped down tunnels or into enclosures, forcing people out into the open. US troops would then move in before the effect of the gas had worn off.[13]

Biological weapons are of little use on the battlefield itself: they are simply too slow. The military today prefer nerve gases because they are quick acting. However, if an attack can be phased over a number of days biological agents might be used to advantage. They could hamper an enemy's advance by weakening troops with some debilitating illness. In this scenario the target would probably be large emplacements of troops, for a large body of soldiers would move less frequently, giving the biological agents time to act. The 1966 US manual for CBW envisaged another situation. Biological weapons, it said, might be used in the preparatory phase of a large-scale attack from air and sea.[14] Contagious agents spread by human contact would not be used on the battlefield; however, they might be released deep behind enemy lines to knock out communications posts, missile positions and military bases.

The logistical requirements needed to service troops fighting in a war where CBW are used are considerable. Protective clothing will need to be available at all times and will either have to be worn or carried. Elaborate preparations will be necessary for servicing weapons and for decontaminating vehicles. Some provisions will have to be made for resting or replacing troops who will tire more easily because of their apparel and the stress of fighting in an environment where chemical weapons are used.[15]

Although the equipment is bound to hamper operations to

some extent, the problems are far fewer than they were 10 years ago. The protective equipment for NATO and Warsaw Pact forces which is available (clothing, respirators, shelters) is similar to that issued for protection against radioactive nuclear weapons. Even those troops required to use radios or perform some skilled visual function will, it is claimed, have little difficulty in carrying out their tasks.[16]

Physiological stresses of wearing the equipment are minor, and psychological problems can be overcome with training. The protective suit issued to US servicemen weighs about 4lb, is water-repellent and permeable to air – it 'breathes', in other words. This reduces heat stress, the main cause of discomfort with earlier versions. At Central European temperatures heat stress will be only a minor problem. At temperatures above 75–80°F, any exertion would probably have to be limited to a few hours at most.

According to two of the world's leading experts on chemical warfare – Professor Matthew Meselson of Harvard University and Julian Perry Robinson at Sussex University – the protective clothing issued to Russian soldiers is reported to be made of an airtight rubberised fabric. This does not 'breathe' and therefore can be worn for only about four hours at temperatures of 60°F before heat stress occurs. Above 70°F it can be worn for only 30 minutes. Needless to say, the Russians are said to be working on an improved version.[17]

As for gas masks, these are very effective and can be donned in a matter of seconds – they are even comfortable enough to be worn during sleep. The filters in the mask are made of charcoal impregnated with a metal, such as copper, to degrade chemicals. A new mask issued to US troops also has glass fibre to increase the retention of particles. A properly fitted gas mask is said to reduce the concentration of gas which can be inhaled by a factor of at least 100,000. Charcoal is also used on the inner lining of protective suits. Any vapour which penetrates the outer layers – a wettable surface designed to increase the rate of evaporation of nerve agents – will be absorbed by the charcoal.

As far as protection for vehicles is concerned, the latest Russian and Warsaw Pact tanks have protective seals and are fitted with positive pressure filter-air supplies so that crews are fully protected without having to wear masks. The Russians appear to favour this system for troop-carrying vehicles, whereas the US armoured personnel carriers have a central supply of air to which individual respirators can be attached; this allows soldiers to enter and leave the vehicle without difficulty.[18]

It is worth remembering that a dose of nerve gas sufficient to cause casualties will be inhaled before anyone experiences the classic symptoms of poisoning – a runny nose, deteriorating vision and tightness in the chest. In view of this, alarms to detect nerve agents on the battlefield need to be extremely sensitive. Automatic field alarms are now available which mimic the action of nerve gas in the body, causing a fall in concentration of a chemical – thiocholine – which triggers the alarm. In addition to the automated devices, individual soldiers have strips of detection paper on the arm, wrist and ankle of their protective suits.

The first and most effective line of defence against chemicals is protective clothing. A second line is the self-administered antidote. These would be used if troops were inadvertently exposed to nerve gas before they had time to don protective equipment. The antidotes – atropine and an oxime – can overcome the effect of the nerve gas. They would be administered by auto-injection as soon as soldiers started to experience any symptoms. Regrettably, however, the antidotes work only if the dose inhaled or absorbed is not too high. In many cases artificial respiration would also be needed to keep the victim alive. On the battlefield the facilities for such treatment are strictly limited. It would appear that the distribution of antidotes serves a more important role as a morale booster – as a life-saver their value is strictly limited.

The third and last line of defence would be to get rid of the agents themselves by some form of decontamination. There are many chemicals which will do this: a bleaching powder is one. According to Meselson and Robinson, the Warsaw Pact countries have invested heavily in this kind of defence. Their troops have large numbers of vehicles which they use for both chemical and radiological decontamination. One such is the TMS-65, a turbo jet large-volume dispenser. Two TMS-65s working together are said to be capable of cleaning the outer surfaces of a tank in three minutes.

Warsaw Pact forces are said to have at least 80,000 troops trained to detect chemicals, give medical aid and to decontaminate vehicles.[19] These troops train routinely during Warsaw Pact manoeuvres. There are some claims that real chemical weapons are used in these exercises. According to John Erickson, Professor of War Studies at Edinburgh University, these training exercises involve the use of lethal chemical weapons so that troops are aware of the dangers of failing to protect themselves from exposure to these agents.[20] NATO sources make similar claims.[21]

As for the US Army, every company of 100–300 soldiers has at least 15 men allocated to chemical detection and decontamination. However, the US is in the process of upgrading its anti-chemical defences and is investing considerable funds to achieve this. Between 1971 and 1976 some $15–20 million was invested annually for the defence of US NATO troops against chemicals. In 1977 this quadrupled, and it is at present $90 million a year. During NATO exercises troops train in protective clothing to familiarise themselves with the conditions they would encounter in a chemical war.

Little of this spending will have much effect on civilians. Only two western countries – Sweden and Switzerland – provide protective equipment and training for their civilian population. Current chemical weapons are not designed for strategic purposes, but for tactical use on the battlefield. The military do not envisage that they will be used intentionally on civilians. But these plans can take no account of adverse weather conditions. Even a light breeze will carry chemicals a long way beyond the battlefield and affect millions of people. As for areas sprayed with persistent chemicals such as VX, these will remain hazardous long after the fighting is over and will be strictly out of bounds to the public.

Meselson and Robinson paint a rather grim picture of what might happen on a battlefield in central Germany.[22] They choose a typical day which is cool, overcast, but dry, with a light breeze blowing from the South-West. A chemical attack is launched in these conditions with the nerve agent sarin, used in concentrations sufficient to cause 20 per cent casualties among soldiers who, caught unawares, are not wearing their respirators. The breeze causes the gas to drift, and any unprotected person up to 15 miles away is killed. People over twice this distance from the battle are seriously injured. The result: millions of casualties. Many of these casualties will require help for life. Death from nerve agents is by asphyxiation. If the concentration of gas is not sufficient to cause death, a person may still be exposed to enough to affect their breathing and deprive them of oxygen for long enough to cause brain damage. Any health service faced with a large number of people so severely disabled will be faced with a terrible burden. Its resources would be stretched to the limit. As for the outer reaches of the gas cloud – which will of course be invisible – people will experience pain in the eyes, headaches, and possibly difficulty in breathing.

Some equally grim scenarios have been painted for the use of biological weapons.[23] A study group of the World Health Organization (WHO) reported in 1970 that the use of biological warfare on a strategic scale was probably impractical; there were too many risks of the attack backfiring.[24] Although a large proportion of the enemy population might be infected, there was a strong possibility that the agent used might change to a more virulent strain. Even though troops of the attacking army would be immunised to the initial agent, they could be vulnerable to the new strain. Once infected, the troops would carry the disease home. Everyone – troops and civilians – would then have been affected. The WHO panel thought, therefore, that biological warfare was more likely to be used in tactical situations against selective military targets.

But just to demonstrate what could happen, the WHO panel considered some possible situations in which an attack against civilians might occur. One example they chose was anthrax. A single bomber could contaminate an area 30km long by 2km wide. Any wind would transport the anthrax organisms even further. If anthrax was to be sprayed over a city in a developed country with a population of 5 million, the panel estimated that it would kill 100,000 people and incapacitate a further 150,000 people. In a city in a developing country where the population density might not be so great, an attack over a city of 5 million would kill 95,000 and incapacitate a further 15,000. Medical treatment with antibiotics would reduce the casualties by 50 per cent in the developed country, but probably only by about 5 per cent in the developing nation. The resources in the poorer country would be insufficient to provide treatment on anything like the scale needed. Even in a developed country there is no certainty that medical resources would be adequate or indeed that there would be sufficient supplies of the right kinds of antibiotic available for treatment: each bacteriological agent has to be treated with a specific medical regime and a wide spectrum of antibiotics would be needed to cater for any eventuality.[25]

Biological weapons might also be used for an attack on a water supply. If, say, the micro-organism causing botulism was introduced into a mains water supply (in a reservoir, the concentration would be too dilute) it could have a devastating effect. Botulism is a deadly infection and its effects in humans are noticeable within 6–8 hours. If the botulinal organism were to be placed in the water supply for a small industrial town of some 50,000 inhabitants it is estimated that 28,000 people would swallow a lethal dose of the bacterium in their drinking water before a general alarm could be raised. By that time the saboteur could be many miles from the scene of the crime and would probably escape detection altogether. The reason for the attack and the perpetrators might never be known.[26]

Physical damage is not the only problem with chemical and biological weapons: there are considerable social repercussions as well. To prevent diseases spreading, the health authorities – aided by the military – might have to introduce harsh measures to keep the population in or out of a particular area. And these measures might have to stay in effect for a long time. Whether or not the authorities could enforce these measures is another question. There is a real possibility that panic amongst the population may be so extensive that restrictions would be ineffectual and the desire for self-preservation would override any appeal to order.[27]

Any country that initiates chemical and biological warfare will be well aware of the effect it will have on public order.

Initiating CBW would be an act of considerable political importance. By ignoring, indeed flouting, international law on the use of these weapons in war, a country caught using them would be inviting grave retribution. But in a war it is military considerations which dominate. Although political repercussions would not be ignored, the prime objective for a country at war would be winning the conflict. In this situation chemical and biological weapons might be used.[28] It is conceivable that nuclear weapons might also be used early in a conflict. NATO has made it clear that it may well resort to the use of nuclear weapons if its defensive positions were overwhelmed by a Russian advance.

What factors might influence the decision to use these weapons? Economics might be one. Chemical weapons were once vaunted as the poor nation's atomic bomb. However, as more nations acquire the potential to make nuclear weapons it seems that the poor nation merely has more diversity in its arsenal. The economic argument has little validity today.

The relationship between personnel and firepower in any conflict is crucial to its outcome. A hundred years ago military strategists could still argue that troop numbers were more important than firepower. In other words, that quantity would prevail over quality. With the mechanisation of warfare this is no longer true. Wars now – and in the future – will be won by the side with the more sophisticated weaponry, as the 1982 Falklands/Malvinas war demonstrated only too clearly. In set-piece battles quality will prevail. Guerilla warfare, on the other hand, is quite different. The Vietnam war proved that technological superiority does not always determine the outcome of a war, and that a stronger-motivated, but less well-equipped army counts for far more than the latest weaponry.

Military strategists have considered situations where a shortfall in troop numbers might be crucial to the outcome of a war. This shortfall might tempt a country to use chemical weapons, a scenario that was once envisaged for a war between the US and China, the latter having huge reserves of trained militia.[29]

There is also the use of chemical weapons for counter-insurgency operations. In guerilla warfare where the attacked force is likely to be small groups, probably travelling light, nerve gases could cause high casualties. Most guerillas would be unlikely to have protective equipment.

As good protection is the best way of deterring chemical warfare, its absence might provide the necessary incentive to actually use it. This situation might be more important for a conflict between a well-endowed nation and a poorer third world country.

A potential war between NATO and Warsaw Pact forces could hardly be described in these terms, however: both sides have good defensive measures against chemical weapons and both advertise this fact as often as possible. NATO's position on the use of chemical weapons is one of 'no first use'. Why then does it retain stocks of these weapons?

According to Meselson and Robinson, the Russians might be dissuaded from initiating chemical warfare during a major conventional attack in Europe by NATO's ability to retaliate in kind. If this deterrence fails, however, NATO use of chemical weapons might at least slow down the Russian advance, leaving both sides handicapped.[30]

The field manual issued to US forces in Europe explains the options succinctly:[31]

> The objective of US policy is to deter the use of chemical weapons by other nations. If this deterrence fails, and the use of chemical weapons is authorized by national command authorities, the primary objective is to achieve early termination of chemical warfare operations at the lowest level of intensity.

How realistic is this hope? Are NATO's chemical weapons a deterrent? Or could their use escalate a conflict? Regrettably, the answer to the latter question is 'yes'. Chemical warfare is likely to be used in addition to conventional warfare and it is certain to make conditions on the battlefield a good deal worse. By aggravating the effects of a conventional attack, chemical weapons could make nuclear warfare more likely. But could chemical weapons have any deterrent value? The answer would seem to be 'very little'. The presence of chemical weapons in the arsenals of NATO and the Warsaw Pact only serves to heighten tension and makes war more likely.

Most NATO countries still appear reluctant to divert large resources into the procurement of chemical weapons. It is only the US which is pressing for the production of binary nerve gas weapons. Most of these, according to US calculations, will be destined for Europe. At the moment, however, many NATO countries are still unwilling to store chemical weapons. Europe still remembers with horror the effect of chemical warfare in the First World War.

The appalling suffering these weapons caused was not matched by any significant strategic gain by the military of either side. The result was a stalemate. If chemical weapons were used again and their use did not precipitate a nuclear conflict, this situation might be repeated. This time, however, there would be millions of civilian casualties to add to those of the armed forces. To prevent this happening, the best approach would be to make sure that chemical weapons are not used. For this, we need recourse to popular movements of protest – and to the law.

6. The law

Chemical and biological warfare (CBW) is prohibited by international law. Two treaties forbid it. The 1925 Geneva Protocol outlaws the use of chemical and biological weapons. But the Protocol does not deny countries the right to have these weapons. That right, as far as stockpiles of biological weapons are concerned, is now forbidden by the 1972 Biological Weapons Convention. No such convention exists for chemical weapons.

The Geneva Protocol was drawn up largely at the insistence of the USA. Conceived as a means of regulating the conduct of warfare, the Protocol was an attempt to make explicit a declaration banning chemical weapons issued 60 years earlier. That declaration, drawn up in the Russian capital of St Petersburg in 1868, called on nations to renounce the use of projectiles 'charged with fulminating or inflammable substances'.[1] This text became more specific in a convention signed by the world powers attending the First International Peace Conference in the Hague in 1899. Signatories to the convention agreed in the interests of humanity to 'abstain from the use of projectiles, the object of which is the diffusion of asphyxiating or deleterious gases'.[2]

Unfortunately, events were to prove that this declaration had loopholes. When German troops used chlorine gas at Ypres in 1915 the gas was released from cylinders hidden in trenches. The fact that 'projectiles' had not been used to release the gas led Germany to claim that the Hague Convention had not been violated. Technically, this was correct, but the spirit of the Hague agreement had clearly been broken.

The suffering caused by the use of poison gas in the fields of France and Flanders removed any doubts about the need for an effective agreement to outlaw chemical warfare. Those who drafted the Geneva Protocol were aware of this, and they prepared a text which was both simple and comprehensive. The 1925 Protocol outlaws 'the use in war of asphyxiating, poisonous or other gases, and of all liquids, materials and devices'.[3] It also prohibits bacteriological (biological) warfare.

About 100 states have signed the Protocol, including all members of the Warsaw Pact and NATO. Asian states said to have used chemical weapons in the past, or alleged to have used them more recently, are also signatories – including Japan, Vietnam and Laos. A victim of chemical warfare, China, has also signed. Kampuchea, however, has not.[4] Even though some nations are still not party to the Protocol they are nevertheless affected by it. The prohibitions of the treaty are now considered to have entered customary international law. In other words, whenever there is a war it is the recognised custom that chemical weapons will not be used. And this sanction applies not only to those who have actually signed the Protocol, but to everyone else as well.

Just over one-third of the countries party to the Protocol have reserved the right to retaliate in kind. This reservation allows them to keep stockpiles of chemical weapons ostensibly for defensive purposes. Views between members of NATO and the Warsaw Pact differ on the need for this reservation.[5] As Table 5 (p. 123) shows, countries within these two alliances are almost equally divided on this point. There is some doubt, too, about the value of these reservations. Under the rules governing conduct in warfare in general, belligerents are allowed to conduct reprisals in kind. This right has considerable deterrent value. Combatants are usually unwilling to initiate particularly barbarous acts if they know that reprisals of a similar nature are likely to be used against them. The reservations to the Geneva Protocol are not necessary to guarantee the right of retaliation; this is already guaranteed.

Even if attacked with chemical weapons, signatories to the Protocol are not guaranteed the right to escalate a chemical warfare conflict at will. They would be expected only to retaliate in kind and in due proportion, against the first user. Anything else would be seen to be a violation of the aims of the Protocol.

Thus the reservations do not seem to confer any more rights than are already allowed for reprisals in kind.[6]

By announcing that they insist on the right to retaliate in kind with chemical weapons, countries are in effect serving notice that they are likely to have stockpiles of these weapons. Unfortunately, the law notwithstanding, the mere possession of these stocks makes their use that much more likely.

There have been only three confirmed violations of the Geneva Protocol. The first was the use of mustard gas by Italy in the Ethiopian campaign of 1935–6;[7] the second was the use of mustard gas and Lewisite by Japan against China between 1937 and 1945;[8] and the third was the use of herbicides and incapacitants by the US in Vietnam from 1962 to 1971.[9] In the first two of these violations there was no question that the Protocol had been broken: both Italy and Japan used traditional chemical weapons to harry their opponents. As regards the third violation, however, it has long been the view of the US that herbicides and incapacitants were not covered by the Protocol. When the US belatedly ratified the Protocol in 1975 – 50 years after its constitution – it did so without referring to herbicides, merely adding the qualification that the US reserved the right to retaliate in kind if attacked with chemical weapons. Since then, however, the US has let it be known that it does not consider herbicides and riot-control agents to be covered by the Geneva Protocol. Nevertheless, the US has renounced the use of these agents in war except for three or four specific kinds of situation.[10] Herbicides, for example, may still be used to clear vegetation around US military base camps.

The US is not alone in its view that some chemical agents are outside the scope of the Protocol. Britain now subscribes to the view that the riot-control agent CS is not covered. In February 1970, when the British government reversed its previous position and announced that CS was not covered by the Protocol, it was probably trying to forestall criticism of its use of this gas in Northern Ireland.[11]

It is on grounds of toxicity that Britain believes that CS is exempt from the Protocol. The gas, Britain says, is relatively non-toxic. To complicate the issue further, CS is used domestically as an anti-riot agent. Many countries use it for this purpose and television viewers are familiar with the use of the gas in riots on the streets of Chicago, Tokyo, Warsaw and Paris. Because anti-riot gas is used at home, the US claims that it cannot be covered by the Protocol. This view was made explicit by the US delegate at the First Committee of the United Nations General Assembly in 1966. The delegate maintained[12] that the Protocol

does not apply to all gases, and it certainly does not prohibit the use of simple tear gas . . . It is unreasonable to contend that any rule or international law prohibits the use in military combat against an enemy of non-toxic chemical agents that governments around the world commonly use to control riots by their own people.

On the face of it this is a rather specious argument. Domestic conflicts and international wars are not the same thing. Governments can be brought to book by their own citizens for infringements of domestic human rights. In an international war this sanction is absent. All the more reason, therefore, why there should be a certain code of conduct for the prosecution of war. This is a view which is accepted by the majority of the members of the UN for, in 1969, with a vote of 80 to 3 with 36 abstentions, resolution 2603A was passed by the General Assembly declaring that the use of '*any chemical agents of warfare*' was 'contrary to the generally recognised rules of international law, as embodied in the [Geneva Protocol].' Those voting against were Australia, Portugal and the US (not party to the Protocol at the time). Britain abstained on the motion.[13]

Although party to the Geneva Protocol, a few countries are also subject to treaty restrictions on possession of chemical weapons under the terms of their Second World War peace treaties and subsequent declarations. Those affected include West Germany, Bulgaria, Hungary, Italy and Rumania.[14]

To make the ban on chemical weapons universal, and thus to further strengthen the Geneva Protocol, talks between governments on chemical and biological disarmament began in 1968, within the Geneva Conference of the Committee on Disarmament (CCD). (In 1978 the CCD was reformed and expanded to become the 40-Nation Committee on Disarmament (CD).) Progress in these talks on CBW disarmament was mixed: there was greater support for the need to eliminate biological weapons than for similar strictures on chemical ones. In 1971, therefore, the CCD split the two subjects and began separate negotiations for a ban on biological weapons. A biological warfare disarmament treaty emerged swiftly from these negotiations. This treaty, the 1972 Biological Weapons Convention, entered into force on 26 March 1975: parties to it undertake never to 'develop, produce, stockpile' or retain 'biological agents, or toxins, whatever their origin or method of production' in quantities which have no justification other than for defence, or for the treatment of disease. Signatories agree never to use these weapons in armed conflict. The Convention also contains a commitment by the parties concerned to continue negotiations in 'good faith' for a complementary chemical weapons convention.[15]

These negotiations did not continue immediately. It was four years before the first substantive moves were made. Britain tabled a draft convention at the CCD in 1976.[16] The British draft was seen by many countries as a welcome move in the direction of achieving a comprehensive chemical weapons treaty. Events stemmed their optimism. In 1977 the USA and USSR established a working group in which they could talk privately to each other. This move effectively isolated the normal negotiating forum – the CCD in Geneva – many of whose members are European countries who have a great deal more at stake in a CW treaty than do the superpowers. Not surprisingly, many governments were angry. To reduce the tension a compromise was reached in 1980 between the superpowers and the other members of the Committee on Disarmament. It was agreed to establish an *ad hoc* working group 'to define, through substantive examinations, issues to be dealt with in the negotiations on' a CW convention. But this was a poor compromise. The ability of the superpowers to render even this modest agreement ineffective was clearly illustrated in 1981 when the USA, under the new Reagan administration, both declined to resume bilateral negotiations with the Russians and – though this was at least as much the fault of the USSR – continued to deny the Geneva Disarmament Committee a proper negotiating mandate.[17]

With the advent of the Reagan administration, disarmament negotiations reached a new low. Prior to this, and in spite of the turmoil created by the Soviet intervention in Afghanistan, the bilateral US–Soviet negotiations had made a good deal of progress.

US and some NATO leaders claim that the Russians would not accept the principle of verification by on-site inspection.[18] Naturally, for any treaty to be successful there would have to be provisions for checking possible violations of both the manufacture and use of chemical weapons. Everyone accepts this. Nevertheless, this is what the US delegate to the European Security Conference Meeting in Madrid in February 1982 had to say: 'We found that the Soviet Union rejected all suggestions for on-site inspection'.[19] The British government's view is contained in a document, *Peace and Disarmament*, published in January 1982. This states that[20]

[whereas] Western States have offered to accept all kinds of verification measures necessary to ensure that parties to arms control agreements are not cheating, the Soviet Union has traditionally rejected them, and in particular has resisted any sort of on-site inspection arrangements.

Contrast these statements with the agreed joint report issued by the US and USSR on the progress made in their bilateral negotiations in Geneva on a chemical weapons ban. The report, summarising developments at the tenth series of bilateral talks, speaks of the right for any party to a CW convention to request 'investigation of the actual state of affairs on-site'.[21] It continues: 'A party may agree to such an on-site investigation or decide otherwise, providing appropriate explanations.' Although this text may allow for some prevarication on the part of a country suspicious of the reasons for an on-site visit, it does indicate that the USSR is agreed, at least in principle, to some kind of inspection facility to make a CW treaty workable.

To add substance to this principle Foreign Minister Andrei Gromyko submitted a draft text for a convention outlawing the possession of chemical weapons at the United Nations Special Session on Disarmament in New York in June 1982. The Soviet proposition is that all types of chemical weapons be banned in war, that present stocks of these weapons be destroyed, and that provisions be made on both a national and international basis to ensure compliance with the convention. Provisions should be made, the Sovet Union says, for on-site inspection.[22]

Thus, once again, the Russians are saying that on-site inspection need not prevent agreement on a chemical warfare treaty. The Soviet Union has clearly conceded some ground. Previously it had not been prepared to admit use of the verification technique to the extent that the Americans, and more particularly the British, were demanding.[23] (Curiously, the US and Soviet positions are the reverse of what they were 50 years ago. In the early 1930s the US opposed supervision, arguing that disarmament must rest on good faith. The Soviet Union, on the other hand, stressed in its disarmament plan of March 1928 that there should be open supervision and inspection of sites.)[24]

The Russians have made much political capital out of American prevarications – but so far the US government has made no move to reopen negotiations. A vote in the US House of Representatives to block funds for the production of binary nerve gas weapons in 1982 did not alter the government's stance. On 22 July the House of Representatives voted 251 to 159 to approve an amendment to the Defense Authorization Bill withdrawing the $54 million earmarked for the production of binary chemical weapons in the fiscal year 1983.[25] Two weeks previously Senate had approved this funding by 49 votes to 45. The Congress vote effectively blocked funds for the production of binary nerve gas weapons, but left, virtually untouched, funds for research and development in this area.

On 12 August 1982 a Senate House Conference Committee met to resolve the conflicting votes on this issue and decided to approve the Senate vote. But the following day, 13 August 1982, this decision was reversed and it was finally resolved to block the funds for binary production. In voting to block the funds, the House of Representatives called on President Reagan to promote negotiations on chemical weapons among members of the *ad hoc* working group of the Geneva Disarmament Committee in order 'to draft a treaty prohibiting such weapons'.

Many members of Congress felt sure that the US administration would not accept this defeat and that an attempt would be made to retrieve the situation when the budget for the fiscal year 1984 was considered. This, in fact, is what has happened.

Congress was asked to approve a chemical weapons budget of $792 million, of which $195 million was for a 'retaliatory program' to produce new weapons – the Bigeye bomb and a binary 155mm artillery shell. In addition, the US Department of Defense had asked Congress to reinstate a cut made in the 1983 allocation. The request for Bigeye money was withdrawn before Congress voted on the matter because of a problem in its development. On 16 June 1983 the House of Representatives voted by a large majority *not* to authorise money to begin making binary artillery shells. One month later, in July 1983, the Senate voted 50 to 49 to *approve* the request through the casting vote of George Bush: 1983 was turning into a replay of the events in 1982, with the nerve gas matter going before a congressional conference committee. In August the joint House–Senate committee met and approved the money for binaries; this was carried through the authorisation stage in the House on 15 September. So, in addition to the $0.8 billion for chemical weapons defence and research, $115 million has now been authorised for the production of the binary 155mm artillery shell in the recently-built factory at Pine Bluff, Arkansas, and to start setting up new plant for Bigeye. Production will not start before 1985 and then only if the president certifies that it is in the national interest. Congress has made one proviso. These new munitions must *replace* existing stocks – shell for shell, bomb for bomb.

President Reagan is clearly determined to have this money for binaries which he sees as an integral part of the government's defence policy. Senior officials in the US Department of Defense, as well as the present NATO Supreme Commander General Bernard Rogers, portray the binary programme as a 'bargaining chip' to be used in future disarmament negotiations.[26] The US has argued that an effective chemical warfare treaty cannot be negotiated from a position of weakness and that current NATO stocks of chemical weapons are inadequate to deter a chemical attack by Warsaw Pact countries.[27]

As for relying on the threat that nuclear weapons might be

used by NATO in response to a Soviet attack with chemical weapons, there are those in NATO who argue that this is not realistic. They cite two reasons. First, it is too rigid and predictable and therefore runs counter to NATO's 'flexible response' strategy. Second, it would lower the nuclear threshold, an outcome everyone believes to be undesirable.[28] For these reasons the US believes it needs its binary programme. However, the position has changed a little in the last year. In spite of US allegations about its use of chemicals in Indo-China and Afghanistan, the USSR appears willing to negotiate a chemical warfare convention – *before* the US acquires binary weapons. The question must then be asked: 'Does the US really need them?' All the evidence would suggest that by building these weapons the US would be fuelling a chemical arms race.

Binary weapons will create considerable difficulties for those negotiating a verifiable chemical weapons convention. As the two separate chemical components of the weapons are essentially non-toxic, their manufacture is a relatively simple process and one that could be carried out by any number of small chemical companies used to handling toxic chemicals. In December 1981, the US Army asked chemical producers if they would be willing to produce the component chemicals for the binary weapon. Although larger chemical companies – such as American Cyanamid, Monsanto, Ethyl and Mobil Chemical – said they were not interested in the proposal, some smaller companies were most keen. Two of these – Speciality Organics (of Irwindale, California) and Synathatron (of New Jersey) – specialise in the manufacture of toxic and corrosive gases and liquids: both said they would tender for the contract. Speciality Organics has expertise in the field of organophosphorus chemistry – the basis of nerve gases. Neither of these smaller companies appeared to be concerned about any adverse publicity arising out of their involvement. The prospect of bad publicity, however, was one of the principal reasons why the larger companies said no.[29]

There is more than publicity or profits at stake with binary weapons as far as the Committee on Disarmament is concerned. Many members of the committee are convinced that binary weapons will not only delay agreement on a chemical weapons treaty but could well prevent one ever being agreed. There are several reasons for this. First, it will be extremely difficult to monitor – or police – all private manufacturers involved in the production of binary nerve gases. Second, many of the individual chemicals used to make nerve gases are used widely throughout the chemical industry. Keeping tabs on these will be immensely difficult.

With the current generation of nerve gas weapons, the actual loading of the weapon has always been a problem. The nerve agent is lethal and jeopardises the safety of those handling the weapon. In addition, facilities for stockpiling the weapons in remote locations – where they can do the least harm if leakage occurs – are also required. Such sites would be few in number, and monitoring a simpler process. With binary weapons the opposite is true. They are dangerous only when their two components mix on firing. As the shells would be stockpiled with just one component, their siting is not problematic. Detecting these sites, however, could be. The task of inspection teams monitoring a chemical weapons treaty would be difficult.

Given the situation, is there any chance of securing a ban on the use of chemical weapons? And how long will it take to reach an agreement? The answer to the first question must be guardedly optimistic because of progress made recently at the CD in Geneva. In public the US government has indulged in some sabre-rattling over chemical weapons. In private, however, US negotiators in Geneva have been setting out their requirements for the chemical weapons treaty.[30] The significant feature about the US proposals is that they do not differ substantially from those presented by Foreign Minister Andrei Gromyko at the UN on 16 June 1982.[31] Both superpowers agree that super-toxic lethal chemicals should not be used in warfare. They also agree that riot-control agents should be permitted for law enforcement purposes. The US, however, is still insisting that herbicides should not be covered by the treaty.[32]

The US and the USSR also agree on the need for a verification procedure to police a chemical warfare treaty. It is the details of this procedure which need to be finalised and these will have to be discussed at the CD's *ad hoc* working group on chemical weapons. The working group has already tackled this problem and at its session on 17–28 January 1983 it addressed itself to issues such as the procedures for monitoring the destruction of chemical weapons stockpiles; the need to destroy chemical weapon manufacturing plant or oversee its conversion for other uses; ensuring that chemical weapons are not made in future; and the destruction of incinerator plants, and the like, built for the express purpose of destroying chemical weapons. In addition, the group discussed requirements for an international inspectorate that could investigate sites where chemical warfare was alleged to have been waged.[33]

It was this measure of agreement between most nations which prompted a British Foreign Office minister, Douglas Hurd, to address the CD on 10 March 1983 in an optimistic vein.[34] In describing the CD as a 'unique negotiating forum', he outlined a procedure for securing a chemical weapons treaty. It should, he said, be a step-by-step process, and, as a first step,

> we need to step back from our detailed discussions to analyse what is really important in this field. The most important and immediate task is to rid the world of the existing arsenals of chemical weapons. We might begin with substances in the super-toxic category – of which by far the most important are the so-called nerve gases. No one can contemplate their use without revulsion.

Mr Hurd then went on to suggest a less stringent verification procedure for less toxic chemicals, such as the First World War chemical gases phosgene and hydrogen cyanide. Many of these are used widely in the chemical industry as intermediates and monitoring them closely would necessitate policing the civil chemical industries of the world. 'We cannot and should not want to police these in detail,' said Mr Hurd, 'when good progress can be made on focusing on the products of a very narrow sector [i.e. the super-toxic chemicals].'

At the same time, Mr Hurd presented the CD with a technical paper in which it is made clear that Britain's chemical industry does not envisage any problems in adhering to a verification procedure of the sort he outlined.[35] The British proposals at the

CD on 10 March have been well received. In effect, Britain is saying that the nations at the CD should recognise the areas on which they agree, but not be deflected by differences of detail on some issues. This would seem to be a realistic basis on which to proceed. It should be possible to secure a treaty which, although not necessarily all-embracing at the beginning, could become so in the future – after more detailed discussions – when it was clear that the initial restrictions were being observed.

Suggestions have also been made that Europe should be declared a 'chemical-free' zone. This has been suggested by both the Palme Commission[36] and by the leaders of the Warsaw Pact in the statement issued after the January 1983 Prague Summit.[37] Many feel that such a step could do no harm and that it would hasten the process of chemical disarmament.

Declarations, however, are one thing; achieving a chemical-free Europe might be more difficult. A procedure of verification would still be required to ensure that European nations were abiding by their declarations; agreeing on such a procedure would probably only divert attention away from the need to secure a comprehensive chemical weapons treaty that would apply worldwide.

But this is not to decry declarations of intent not to use chemical weapons. There are still nations which have not yet recognised the 1925 Geneva Protocol on chemical warfare, and this is indeed regrettable. All nations should be encouraged to sign as evidence of their intent to abstain from using chemical weapons. Also, there are some 30 states which ratified the Geneva Protocol, but added the rider that they reserved the right to retaliate in kind with chemicals. The reservation serves one purpose. It provides an excuse to stock chemical weapons. By withdrawing this reservation, countries could signal their intention to have nothing to do with these agents. Ireland has already done this. Others, by taking similar action, can make continued possession of chemical weapons appear increasingly illegitimate. In this way one-third of those states, including Britain, which are party to the Protocol can bring pressure to bear on the super-powers – and on France – to negotiate to achieve effective chemical disarmament.

7. Hands across the sea: the UK–USA alliance

Co-operation in military affairs – at all levels, from weapons research to field operation – has characterised this century's UK–USA alliance. Britain desperately needed industrial capacity in the two major European wars, and the USA openly, but reluctantly, provided it in 1917 and again in 1941 (though for some years before the US had been providing material covertly). Britain also had to pay a price: compliance in the Korean war in the 1950s, in the Indo-China war of the 1960s and 1970s, and an acceptance of US-dominated NATO policy for the 'security of Europe' since 1945. At no time has this been more apparent than in the years since 1979. US-produced medium-range missiles are destined for operational bases in a number of countries of Western Europe. Lying a few miles off the continent of Europe, the UK is the USA's biggest aircraft carrier and is undergoing a period of refitting with conventional, atomic and chemical weaponry.

Anglo–American links in CBW can be traced back to the closing phase of the 1914–18 war when the chemical warfare establishment at Porton Down, and its twin, Edgewood Arsenal in Maryland, were founded. For the next 20 years, irrespective of the 1925 Geneva Protocol, there was continual interchange and exchange. When the twin biological weapons establishments were set up in the early 1940s at Porton and Fort Detrick (Maryland), the alliance was complete and covered all aspects of CBW. The anthrax trials conducted on Gruinard Island, Scotland, in 1942 were attended by American officers.[1] Between 1942 and 1945 the US provided the much-needed personnel and resources ($40 million) to develop biological weapons, in particular the anthrax bomb factory at Vigo, Indiana. The initial work on defoliants had been carried out at ICI in the early 1940s, but because of lack of resources the entire technology was turned over to the US in April 1944. Even Porton Down's tropical research stations in Australia and India were offered for large-scale testing.

Earlier we commented on the fact that chemical weapons were used between 1939 and 1945 on only one front – in China by the Japanese. British research and US capital and industrial capacity had resulted, however, in the potential to unleash devastating weapons upon Germany and Japan. It is probably due to US influence in the closing stages of that war, and particularly to Franklin Roosevelt, that Churchill and the Joint Planning Staff were dissuaded from the use of chemical and biological weapons – but then, of course, the ultimate weapon had been developed and tested at Los Alamos.

For the Allies, the period just after the German and Japanese surrenders was one of revelation. The secrets of German nerve gas research and production were shared, as were the details of the Japanese biological experiments which have only recently come to public light. In 1945 attention focused on Eastern Europe: the advancing Red Army had captured nerve gas plant during its sweep West and had discovered much about biological weapons from Japanese prisoners-of-war taken on the eastern front. Collaboration on chemical and biological weapons continued between the US, Britain and Canada. There was particular interest in biological agents. Late in 1948, Royal Navy ships carrying British, Canadian and US scientists took part in an operation in the Caribbean to test germ weapons. Two similar exercises are reported to have taken place in 1953 and 1954.[2]

By the 1950s, developments in CBW were divided between Britain, the USA, Canada and Australia in a formal quadripartite agreement. British attention had turned to ostensibly defensive research (but note the discovery of the V agents, see p. 13). The USA, with its numerous production facilities, was responsible for weapons development (e.g. VX). Australia and Canada's vast areas of uninhabited land provided suitable testing grounds (Innisfail, Queensland, and Suffield, Alberta, respectively). Though all remaining British stocks of CBW were dumped in the late 1950s, it was on the understanding that supplies of US weapons would be made available if needed.[3] By 1969 all US production of chemical and biological agents had ceased, and within a few years all production facilities and stockpiles of biological agents had been destroyed.[4]

Unhappily this was not the end of the alliance. The chemical and microbiological establishments at Porton Down remain in close contact with their counterparts in the USA. At another level, British and American troops are frequently seen training in anti-gas suits on NATO exercises in scenarios that simulate a gas attack either on or initiated by friendly forces. The alliance is particularly strong between the relevant defence departments. Mounting pressure from the US Chemical Corps has brought chemical weapons production back into US military planning. The funding that has so far been approved, and indeed the programme as a whole, is based on the expectation that a European NATO ally will be found to play host to these new binary weapons. Top of the list is Britain.

What evidence is there of British involvement in this new US venture? The tradition of secrecy in defence matters means that little enters the public record in Britain. However, as one expert on chemical weapons has recently put it: '*any* signs of official interest that reach the public could well mean not only positive support for a CW build-up but also the imminence, even the passage, of decision.'[5]

In June 1979 the (British) government told parliament that it had no plans to equip British forces with chemical weapons;[6] one year later this was reiterated.[7] However, in that period the defence secretary (then Francis Pym) had announced that his department was considering the possibility of a British retaliatory chemical warfare capability.[8] Prime Minister Thatcher confirmed, in June 1980, that she and US Defense Secretary Dr Harold Brown had, that month, discussed the Soviet chemical weapons threat during a visit to London.[9] Mr Pym was reported to have initiated talks with the USA – at the level of military officers and scientists – on how best the two countries could deter Soviet chemical warfare.[10] The implication was that Britain was actively supporting US initiatives. A press report quoting Washington

sources (though denied in London) stated that the British partici-
pants in the talks had a mandate authorising them to discuss
co-production of chemical weapons.[11] In early January 1981,
John Nott replaced Francis Pym as defence secretary. Later that
month, in reply to a question in parliament, it was stated that no
request had been received from the US concerning the basing of
chemical weapons in the UK and that the government had no
plans to store such weapons. A few days later, President Reagan
announced his budget request for 1981–2, which included a sum
specifically for equipping the newly-built binary production
plant at Pine Bluff, Arkansas.

Time after time, parliament has been told that the government
has no plans for British chemical weapons armament. In fact, the
policy not to maintain a chemical weapons capability has been
endorsed by the last six governments, *but the policy is reviewed
every two years.* Consequently, each statement by the government is carefully worded in the present tense, carrying no commitment for the future. This contrasts with the statement that the
government made on biological weapons in April 1980: 'The
position of the UK remains that in no circumstances would we
consider developing, possessing or using biological weapons.'[12]

In chapter 2, we indicated the types of binary munition currently under consideration by the US. One of these is the so-
called 'Bigeye' bomb, a 500lb spraybomb designed to fit F-4 and
F-111 strike aircraft. The F-111 swing-wing bombers are based at
two USAAF bases in Britain – Lakenheath, Suffolk, and Upper
Heyford, Oxfordshire. At the very end of 1981 Amoretta Hoeber,
Deputy Assistant Secretary for the US Army, told Reuters news
agency in Washington that the Defense Science Board wanted
this new kind of nerve gas bomb to be deployed on US Air Force
bases in Britain. She added that the decision was partly because
of concern that West Germany would not allow them. She went
on to explain that the most compelling reason was that US aircraft
based in England could strike at the rear of Soviet forces in
Europe, whereas nerve gas artillery shells in Germany could be
fired only about 20 miles.[13] The Pentagon would not confirm the
Reuters report and there was much embarrassment on both sides
of the Atlantic. UK Defence Secretary Nott denied any approach

about the deployment of chemical weapons and stated that an approach was not expected. A month later Reagan revealed his budget request for fiscal year 1983 which contained a sum for setting up a fill-line specifically for the Bigeye bomb. As mentioned in chapter 6, this was voted down in Congress, but reappeared as part of a reprogramming request for Congress to consider again in 1983.

Apart from the Bigeye bomb there are other weapons planned to carry binary munitions. All of these have relevance for European governments; two are especially relevant to Britain. The first is the intermediate-range cruise missile. The British government has agreed to accept 160 ground-launched missiles to be stationed at US bases at Greenham Common (Berkshire) and at Molesworth (Cambridgeshire). These missiles, with a range of 2,500km, can carry atomic or binary nerve gas warheads.[14] On 20 January 1981, Philip Goodhart, then Parliamentary Under-Secretary of State for Defence for the Army, in a written reply to Frank Allaun, MP, stated: 'There has never been any suggestion that the 160 cruise missiles to be based in the UK as part of NATO's modernisation of its long-range theatre nuclear forces should have chemical warheads.' Note that this reply is carefully worded. There is no commitment for the future.

The second weapon is the Multiple Launch Rocket System. This weapon is the result of a collaborative development between Britain, the USA, France and Germany. The rocket warhead is designed to take, in addition to others, a binary nerve gas munition. Their full-scale development is imminent.[15]

In 1979, it became clear that a new wave of chemical weapons production was being planned in the USA. This programme has been costed at $10 billion over a 10-year period. In successive years from 1980 there have been budget requests for first a binary factory (approved), and equipment for the factory (approved), then production money for binary munitions (not approved), and most recently for binary munitions again. Currently the US chemical weapons budget requirement is running at one *billion* dollars a year, one-fifth of that being for the retaliatory programme.

At no time since it became clear that the US was embarking

upon a binary weapons programme has there been one word of dissent from the British government. On 7 November 1980, Secretary of State for Defence Francis Pym stated in parliament: 'Whether the United States eventually decides to manufacture new chemical weapons is a matter for the US government.'[16]

But this cannot be so. The types of weapon being developed are, at most, of intermediate range (up to 2,500km) and most are artillery rounds. For use, these weapons must be deployed in Europe and that means a NATO ally. Britain has 150 US military bases and facilities,[17] with 25,000 US Army, Navy and Air Force personnel, and more scheduled to arrive each year.

British troops are equipped with weapons that are designed to take nerve gas munitions. Britain has bases with storage facilities for US weapons and is currently negotiating the purchase of Trident to replace the Polaris system. This purchase, if it is to be on favourable terms, might include a clause about accepting binary nerve gas munitions.

While Britain has always played a major role in CBW disarmament negotiations, from the 1925 Geneva Protocol to the present Geneva talks, it has yet to make a clear commitment to outlaw chemical weapons. Under the Geneva Protocol, the UK retains the right to retaliate in kind were it to be attacked with poison gas; therefore Britain could legally maintain a stockpile of chemical weapons.

In 1982 the Labour Party, with over a two-thirds majority, adopted the following composite resolution at its annual conference in Blackpool:[18]

Conference notes the acceleration of the arms race over the past year and further calls upon the next Labour government to oppose the deployment of chemical and biological weapons in or by Britain.

8. Developments in chemical and biological weapons

The history of the appearance of chemical and biological agents in military arsenals reads like an outdated science fiction novel overtaken by events. Things that were once confined to the imagination of fantasy scriptwriters all too rapidly entered the realms of military possibility. Unhappily, the appearance of new weapons systems this century has been directly linked with progress in science and technology. Research endeavour in the medical and pharmacological fields brings the possibility of new drugs and new treatments. Equally, these new developments can be turned into weapons. While many countries pursue research in the medical field and in chemical industry funded by public money (from shareholders or taxpayers), governments also provide money for defence research. This may involve high-security establishments (such as Porton Down) or may be made available to individuals working in open establishments such as universities and research units. Scientists and technologists are therefore employed directly or indirectly to meet the requirements of the military. Many governments justify research into chemical and biological weapons with the statement that protective measures are being sought. But is it possible to separate 'defensive' from 'offensive' research?

When chlorine was first used in the 1914–18 war the immediate response from the British government was to assemble the 'Special Companies', comprised of science graduates and industrial chemists brought together to develop retaliatory weapons and protective measures. After the war many of them became key figures in ICI or carried on at Porton Down. The same was true in the USA. Scientists were recruited into the growing number of military installations that specialised in the design, first of chemical and then of biological agents.

In the last 70 years many of these installations have come and gone. With the decision by the British government in 1955 to abandon production of chemical and biological weapons and to destroy existing stocks, the newly opened plant at Nancekuke was gradually wound down (though it took over 20 years!). When, in the late 1960s, Richard Nixon ordered a stop to the production of chemical weapons, many US installations closed down. However, Britain still maintains both chemical and microbiological research establishments at Porton Down, and Fort Detrick in the USA remains one of the largest CBW research establishments in the world.

What goes on in these places? Of Porton, little is known because military research has always been a matter of utmost secrecy in Britain. Because of the more open government in the USA, much more is known of research there.

Research in CBW proceeds along a number of lines. New delivery systems are designed, better ways invented to deliver the agent payload, improvements made to the chemical agent so that it persists for longer. But research also goes on to find more lethal agents, to produce these agents more cheaply and to devise agents with particular characteristics. In the 1950s and 1960s, the US spent time and money on so-called 'ethnic' weapons. The task set was to come up with a biological agent that selectively in-capacitated or killed a particular racial group, leaving others unaffected. Highly specific organisms were also sought that in-fected particular species. This was an extension of the philosophy behind defoliants and crop-destruction agents. If a particular social group depended upon, for instance, pigs, sheep or cattle in their economy, then introducing a disease into the herds would be particularly devastating. On a small scale it is possible to see what could happen: outbreaks of 'foot and mouth' (a virus) in Ireland or England are treated as national emergencies. Recent-ly, the Cubans have accused the US of introducing (via the CIA) 'African swine fever' (a virus) into the country and have claimed that this was responsible for repeated infection of pigs.[1]

Scientific discoveries have repeatedly appended one more

category of weapons to the military list. Insecticide research gave rise to the nerve gases. Work on plant hormones resulted in the defoliants. The discovery of LSD provided the impetus for research on incapacitators. In the last decade much more has been revealed about the functioning of living cells and techniques have been designed that enable the transformation of bacteria into programmable biological production units. While these discoveries have tremendous potential in terms of producing vaccines and other pharmaceutically useful agents, they are also vulnerable to military exploitation. Collectively, these techniques and developments are grouped under the heading 'genetic engineering'.[2]

All cells, be they bacteria or the cells that comprise the human liver, have the ability to grow, divide and secrete substances made inside them. The code responsible for initiating production is contained within the chromosomes of the cell.

Let us take two examples of cells producing particular proteins. Acetylcholinesterase, the target for the nerve gases, is produced by cells within the nervous system. A cell actively producing this protein contains the code for acetylcholinesterase together with the translation mechanism. This particular protein has enzymic activity (see p. 11). Acetycholine, in the presence of acetylcholinesterase, is broken down into its constituents. The nerve gases, by attacking the enzyme, prevent the expression of its activity.

The products of some organisms, while not harmful to the organism itself, may have devastating effects on another organism. Occasionally outbreaks of poisoning occur after eating infected shellfish. One of the substances responsible for causing paralytic poisoning is the protein saxitoxin. This is produced by a micro-organism that forms part of the diet of mussels and clams. Inside the micro-organism there is the genetic code for saxitoxin and the mechanism responsible for translating the code into the toxic protein. Each micro-organism produces only a very small amount of the toxin and these particular micro-organisms are not easy to cultivate in the laboratory. However, if it were possible to take a micro-organism – a bacterium, perhaps – that could be easily cultivated and then to insert into this organism the genetic code for saxitoxin, the result would be a production facility for a highly toxic biological agent that could be used as a weapon. Either the toxin could be spread by releasing the transformed bacteria into the air or water supply, or the toxin produced by the bacteria could be collected, concentrated and turned into an aerosol, for example.

The choice of these two examples has not been fortuitous. There is much military interest in isolating quantities of acetylcholinesterase and saxitoxin by using genetic engineering techniques.

The potential of genetic engineering is enormous. Human hormones, interferons (naturally produced substances that have the potential for reversing the growth of malignant tumours), enzymes for diagnostic and therapeutic purposes – in fact, any protein produced by living organisms that is of medical value can be made in this way. But while there is the possibility of reversing and indeed preventing disease (for vaccines can be made in this way), there is also the potential for creating and spreading disease.

When the possibility of genetic engineering became a solid reality in the late 1960s, the military potential was quickly recognised. Under the 1972 Biological and Toxin Weapons Convention, signatory nations pledge never to produce 'microbial or other biological agents, or toxins, whatever their method of production'. However, these agents can be produced, under the Convention, for 'prophylactic, protective or other peaceful purposes'. So governments can initiate programmes that ultimately produce highly pathogenic organisms, or organisms from which highly toxic substances can be harvested, under the flag of medical or 'protective' research. Is there evidence of any government doing so? For the USA the answer is a resounding 'yes', and there is no doubt that many countries throughout the world are doing the same.

In 1974 the US National Academy of Sciences Committee on Recombinant DNA Molecules announced an embargo on certain lines of research. This was a result of concern about safety measures in laboratories where usually harmless bacteria were being transformed into what could be pathogenic strains; the committee was concerned about the deliberate production of harmful agents. The next year the first UK committee on recombinant DNA safeguards dismissed the problem of possible military use because it fell outside the committee's brief.[3]

Up until April 1980, the US Department of Defense stated that it was not sponsoring recombinant DNA research – but things have changed.

First, the guidelines for this type of research have weakened, as evidenced by the recent approval for a proposal to transform the harmless bacterium *Escherischia coli* (which lives in the human gut) into a strain capable of producing diphtheria toxin.[4]

In addition, the last few years have seen the emergence of renewed military interests in biological research and particularly in genetic engineering. As pointed out recently by Susan Wright and Robert Sinsheimer,[5] US Department of Defense support for basic and applied biological research has increased in *real* terms by 20 per cent in the years between 1980 and 1982. This is compared with a 40 per cent *reduction* in funding for biological research by the US National Institutes of Health. Since 1980, some 15 projects involving the new technology have begun in Department of Defense facilities, universities and private laboratories. These include: work on the anthrax bacillus, on the gonorrhoea bacillus, on trypanosomes (these induce sleeping-sickness), and on two viruses (Rift Valley fever and Dengue-2). In all cases the project is described as being for the purposes of raising vaccines against these organisms.[6]

In September 1980 the US Army Medical Research and Development Command put out to tender contracts for the introduction of the gene for acetylcholinesterase into a bacterium. Apparently, the problem was so important that *six* groups are working on it independently (in the universities of Arizona, Massachusetts, San Francisco, San Diego, Case Western Reserve and at the Weizman Institute in Israel). If this enzyme, the target for the nerve gases, could be isolated in quantity it would then be possible to investigate and perhaps design ways of protecting it against agents like soman and tabun. Of course, it would also be possible to test new agents that might be even better inhibitors of the enzyme. In 1982 the National Academy of Sciences approved a request from the Department of Defense to study mycotoxins,[7] the agents alleged to be used by the Vietnamese in Indo-China.

Many genetic engineers in the US are becoming increasingly worried about the grey area between defensive and offensive research. In 1982, Richard Goldstein, from the Harvard Medical School, and Richard Novick, from the Public Health Research Institute in New York City, proposed that the guidelines on genetic engineering be amended to ban research on the construction of biological weapons by molecular cloning.[8] In reply the US government stated that it had no objection to the amendment but argued for a rewording that would allow genetic engineering for 'defensive' purposes.[9] Richard Goldstein has pointed out that many of the current investigations are concerned with disease–viruses that are extremely rare and esoteric – for example, Rift Valley fever – and therefore preparing vaccines against them is useless in anything other than a military context.

Military exploitation of genetic engineering brings the awesome possibility of once benign micro-organisms being transferred into rampant pathogens and of large-scale production of both known and new toxins. The body's own defences (the immune system) and existing vaccines could be rendered useless by genetically transferring more common infectious agents into novel strains. Releasing these pathogenic organisms would induce outbreaks of – for example – dysentery or influenza in enemy troops, rendering them less efficient on the battlefield. While research into biological agents between 1940 and 1970 was directed towards producing a strategic weapon (e.g. anthrax), the present emphasis is on the production of undercover tactical agents that would slowly debilitate the opposition. It is not at all certain that existing conventions will restrain these developments.

In addition to the expansion of biological weapons technology there are developments in chemical agents. During 1982 it was revealed that the second generation of US binary munitions is likely to be based, not on sarin or VX, but on a new agent that has characteristics between the two.[10] Sarin is highly volatile whereas VX is an oily, more persistent agent. This new agent, known by the code-name EA5774,[11] is probably a modified form of soman. Another line of development is towards agents that induce casualties but are designed not to be fatal. Military employment of these casualty incapacitants would necessitate massive evacuation programmes and the need for extensive medical care units, thus diverting the resources of the enemy. In terms of use as civilian control agents, one reported leading contender is code-named EA5302,[12] a solution of a psychotropic drug related to BZ in a novel irritant liquid code-named EA4923. There are also reports of military interest in aerosol anaesthetics as riot-control agents.[13]

The search for novel agents useful in preventing or combating disease, and the devising of new techniques which will aid that pursuit, may prove medically beneficial. However, it must be recognised by scientist and non-scientist alike that this pursuit will create not only the potential for social good, but also for social control – either from within or from without. The new technology that forms the core of genetic engineering is already, in the US, providing new potential therapeutic agents (such as the hormone insulin and the interferons); but that very same technology is also providing the military with the means to develop new nerve agents and novel ways of waging biological warfare.

9. What to do

Despite the research, the stockpiling and the military bluster, there has been no full-scale use of chemical or biological weapons since the 1914–18 war. Despite all the erosion at the edges and the weasel words of politicians determined to prove that tear gases and defoliants are not covered by the Geneva Protocol, the use of chemical and biological weapons *is* banned by international law and specific conventions. Even more specifically, the development and stockpiling of biological and toxin weapons is banned by the 1972 Convention. Agreement on the banning of chemical weapons seems attainable. This ought to appear as a positive record of success in the containment of at least one very real weapon of mass destruction.

Yet massive new production of nerve gases in the US and stockpiling in Europe is imminent. There are probably as many or more scientists and engineers engaged in CBW research today as at any time since 1914, and new developments in biochemistry and genetic engineering open the door onto a whole new landscape of weapons.

Any sane person must ask why? With so much overkill already available, with the entire nuclear arsenal at their disposal, what on earth do the generals want with more? But strategists work, it appears, a bit on the Everest principle: we must have the weapons because they are there, because they are available, because research makes more possible, because there are political careers and industrial profits to be made out of their manufacture . . .

The consequences of such developments are clear. The escalation of chemical weapons under way in the US, and the obvious planning for chemical conflict which characterises Soviet military thinking, suggest that any future war in Europe *cannot but* be chemical as well as nuclear. It is hard, despite the sophisticated military scenarios that we are offered, really to believe that there can be any significant tactical, let alone strategic, benefit to either side from adding these weapons to the arsenals already available. But we are far beyond the stage where rational argument is adequate to convince the strategists. However the pressure for the binary programme arose, the inexorable conclusion of policies advocated by Reagan, Thatcher and, for that matter, by Mitterrand can only be increased hazard for the people of Europe.

We are no safer for having US chemical arms stored in Britain, or in West Germany. It is arguable, at the least, that if the British government were really convinced that a Soviet chemical attack on Britain was likely, the best defence – and, incidentally, one which would create hundreds of thousands of jobs – would be a massive civil defence and shelter programme. But this is not what we are being offered. On offer is merely another form of Mutual Assured Destruction – *except for* the top military, politicians, bureaucrats, industrialists and scientists whose places in the bunkers, come Armageddon, are guaranteed.

It may seem unduly chauvinist to focus on the increased hazard to the peoples of Britain and Europe as a consequence of the binary policy. After all, many rural guerilla movements throughout the world have had to live with the fear of chemicals being used against them ever since the Italian gas attack on the Ethiopians in the 1930s. Anti-chemical aids – from simple respirators to atropine syringes – are now part of the standard requirements by any liberation movement from its solidarity committees in Europe and the US. And the simple techniques for diminishing the worst effects of tear gas and other lachrymators and irritants have been learned afresh by urban guerillas and demonstrators time and again on the streets, from Derry to Paris and Gdansk.

None the less the logic of the present developments in CW rearmament means that we must focus on the 'European theatre'.

First, we should look at the very specific role and responsibilities of scientists themselves in the development and deployment of this new generation of weapons.

Modern weapons of war are the products of a military–industrial–scientific establishment. The innovations in weapons produced in the 1914–18 war – and not merely the poison gases – were the work of chemists who invented new explosives and helped prolong the conflict by developing new industrial processes (for instance, the Haber nitrogen fixation method designed to make Germany independent of imported fertiliser). The 1939–45 war was the war of the physicists who developed radar and, above all, the atomic bomb. Physicists, electronic and computer engineers have shaped the technology of missiles and anti-missiles, spy satellites and the automated battlefield. Increasingly, biologists and biochemists are becoming militarised too. Many physicists who had worked on the Manhattan (atomic weapons) project during the 1939–45 war switched to biology in its aftermath, including several of the founders of the new molecular biology and genetics which have become so important in the last decades. They made the switch partly because of the intellectual challenge of biology, and partly because physics was so clearly about death while biology seemed to be about life.

The major involvement of biology in warfare became apparent at the time of the Vietnam war, when plant biologists found their discovery, the plant hormones, served as the basis of the US defoliation campaign, and biochemists and physiologists found that laboratory curiosities like CS were now part of major weapons systems. Here was a paradox. On the one hand, the rapid drive forward in new chemical and biological weapons came from scientists searching for fame, and, following the industrialisation of biochemistry and genetics, for profit too. On the other hand, much of the vocal *opposition* to the Indo-China war and the use of the new weapons within it came from the scientists. The late 1960s and early 1970s saw the birth, in the US and Britain especially, of movements of radical scientists opposed to the use of science as an agent of repression at home and imperialism abroad: Science for the People in the US, and the British Society for Social Responsibility in Science. For both these groups, the initial focus of their activity was opposition to the role of science in the Indo-China war. The trigger for the 'hot summer' of student activity in Britain in 1968 was the occupation at Essex

University in protest against a Porton researcher coming to speak to the local chemistry department.

Soon, Indo-China came home: students demonstrating at Berkeley, California, were sprayed with CS from helicopters; in Northern Ireland British troops used CS extensively in the Battle of Bogside. On both sides of the Atlantic, but most extensively in the US, the student movement uncovered the complicity of university science departments with the military. Virtually all researching science departments in US universities turned out to have lucrative research contracts with the US Army, Navy or Air Force (and sometimes with the CIA) to work on the basic science behind the new weapons systems. Protests drove many of these contracts off campus, though often only into private research labs set up near the campuses to handle the projects – the military equivalents of California's silicon valley or Boston's Route 128. Today, with the shortage of other sources of university research funds, the contracts are coming back.

In Britain, most military research was and is done in Ministry of Defence establishments rather than in the universities. However, one consequence of the present Tory government's privatisation policy seems to be an increase in putting out work for the Ministry of Defence. British universities at the last count held some 500 separate MoD contracts. We do not know what many of these are for, as the MoD has refused in parliament to list them, but some are clearly for new studies of CW.* An example is the contract in the department of pharmacology in the University of Manchester to study the mechanisms whereby riot-control agents like CR cause pain.

Such contracts, and the secret research they represent, must be opposed. If scientific research is aimed at the genuine defence of the civilian population, it must be open to both parliamentary

---

*If you work or study at a university or polytechnic and want to find out if your campus has such contracts, it is normally possible. They are usually listed in the annual register or calendar or report that all such institutions publish, even if the contracts are given an anodyne or misleading title. If you do find out about any such contracts, and want advice in interpreting what their implications are, you are welcome to contact one of the authors of this book via the publisher.

scrutiny and the control of the local community in which it is done. Only military and oppressive regimes can benefit from secrecy. In Britain we have examples of how the original atomic bomb programme in the late 1940s and the updating of Polaris in the late 1970s were smuggled through cabinet and parliament by Labour prime ministers. Secret research at the universities – whether military or commercial – is inevitably corrupting of the educational purpose which is, or ought to be, a university's prime function.

But research in the universities, especially in Britain, is only a minor aspect of the new developments. In May 1983 the Chemical Defence Establishment at Porton took out large advertisements in the scientific press for biologists to work at CDE on unspecified research problems. We can only guess what these might be, and how they tie in with the contracts discussed in chapter 8 for genetic engineering work to be done at Fort Detrick and under US university contracts.

New techniques of biotechnology, derived from advances in molecular biology and genetic engineering – gene splicing, the production of 'tailor-made' micro-organisms to synthesise specific substances, immobilised enzyme technology, and so forth – are only in their infancy. They have already been the subject of massive inputs of cash from venture capital, multinationals such as ICI and Unilever and the big pharmaceutical companies, and a fair number of paper millions have been made in quoted values of shares floated by the new biotechnology companies. Many leading molecular biologists have made sideways steps out of the universities and into these new laboratories. Whatever other new species genetic engineering may produce, it has already turned up a new type of bio-entrepreneur.

Radical scientists have criticised these developments both for the potential hazards that the accidental production of new and uncontrollable toxic strains might present and for the new ways they offer for the control and manipulation of humans by a science in the hands of a few whose primary goal is the maximisation of profit. So far, most of these developments have linked biology firmly to the industrial rather than to the military part of the military–industrial complex. In the climate of terror produced by binary weapons and CW rearmament, this situation is quickly changing.

It was against this background that, two years ago, an appeal was launched against chemical weapons. Addressed in particular to scientists, it urged them not to participate in any research associated with the development or production of such weapons. Some 2,000 British scientists, mainly biologists, chemists and medical workers, quickly signed the appeal.

But the demands made by that appeal, and the issues we must address, go far wider than just scientists and the militarisation of their work. The US binary programme is clearly going ahead, and will continue unless there is a rapid growth in the strength of the freeze campaign there. As we have seen, these weapons are intended for the European 'theatre' although it is easy to see them being used to supplement other US imperialist wars abroad. The US is therefore known to want to stockpile the weapons in Europe, either in West Germany or in Britain. Prior to the June 1983 election successive Tory ministers of defence repeatedly told parliament that Britain had not (yet) agreed to any such stockpiling, and, indeed, that none had been formally requested. In fact such a request was made in 1982 – though the US Department of Defense, after having embarrassingly stated publicly that a request *had* been made, later backtracked and declared the statement inoperative.

The Labour Party manifesto for the 1983 election contained a clear pledge that under no circumstances would Labour accede to such a stockpiling request. It need hardly be stated that the Tory manifesto contained no such pledge. As the Tories successfully plant cruise at US bases in Britain, and press ahead, as they are likely to do, with basing neutron bombs here too, the next logical step – and the next 'formal' request they are likely to receive – is to take the binaries. After all, what else can the US do with them?

There is no doubt that we must oppose by all means in our power any such British agreement to take the weapons. We must extend the campaign begun by women at Greenham Common and at Porton. We must demand an unequivocal guarantee from the government that under no circumstances will it either produce its own nerve gas weapons or accede to a request to the stockpiling of US weapons – or their binary constituents. And the veil of secrecy behind which the Ministry of Defence hides its activities from British public or parliamentary scrutiny must be pulled aside.

There is also a role for Britain in any effective CW disarmament negotiation between the USA and USSR. Britain should withdraw its own reservation of the right to retaliate in kind, made when it ratified the 1925 Geneva Protocol. It should resubmit its own 1976 draft chemical weapons convention, revised to incorporate proposals on verification, scope, consultation and confidence-building measures.

In the meantime, we should insist that Europe does not become a theatre for chemical weapons. Such weapons must be banned throughout Europe – east and west – as a step towards global banning. And we urge that similar demands are made of their own governments by citizens – scientists and non-scientists alike – in all the countries of Europe. This is not to say that, once Britain had become a nuclear and chemically disarmed country, we could not consider what ought to be done to defend the population *against* chemical attack from whatever source.

The demands of the movement against chemical weapons are an integral part of the demands made by the European Nuclear Disarmament movement in Europe. Neither side's military forces are yet so committed that the drift could not be reversed. We could even envisage CW disarmament preceding nuclear disarmament.

We urge all who read this book to join us and the many who have already committed themselves in support of these demands, and to help spread them to other European countries, east and west. Together, we can build an unstoppable movement against the weapons.

Tables

Table 1 Chemical agents and their effects

Military category	Common/ code-name	Chemical name	Disseminated as	Effects	Lethal dosage†	Originated from
Harassing agents						
irritants (tear gas)	CN	2-chloracetophenone	aerosol	burning feeling, tears, respiratory difficulty, nausea	11000	USA (1918)
	CS*	2-chlorobenzylidine malononitrile	dispersed powder		25000	UK (1950s)
	CR*	dibenzoxazepine	liquid/aerosol		>25000	UK (1960s)
Casualty agents						
incapacitants	BZ*	3-quinuclidinyl benzilate	aerosol		—	USA (1950s)
poison gas	chlorine	—	vapour	giddiness, disorientation broncho-pneumonia	19000	Germany (1915)
	phosgene	carbonyl chloride	vapour		3200	
	mustard gas*	bis (2-chloroethyl) sulphide	vapour	skin and eye blisters, lung damage, broncho-pneumonia	1500	Germany (1917)
	Lewisite	2-chlorovinyl-dichloroarsine	vapour		1300	USA (1918)
	blood gas	hydrogen cyanide	vapour	respiratory failure	2–5000	France (1915)

Table 1 Chemical agents and their effects *(continued)*

Military category	Common/ code-name	Chemical name	Disseminated as	Effects	Lethal dosage†	Originated from
nerve gas	Tabun* (GA)	ethyl NN-dimethyl-phosphoramide cyanidate	vapour/liquid	sweating, vomiting, cramps, chest tightness, coma, convulsion, death from asphyxiation	400	Germany (1936)
	Sarin* (GB)	iso-propyl-methyl-phosphoro-fluoridate	vapour/liquid		100	Germany (1937)
	Soman* (GD)	1,2,2-trimethylpropyl methylphosphoro-fluoridate	vapour/liquid		50	Germany (1944)
	VX*	ethyl S-2-diisopropyl-aminoethyl methylphosphoro-thiolate	liquid/aerosol		10	UK (1952)
incendiaries	napalm*		petroleum fuel plus rubber/ polystyrene	extensive burns, and asphyxiation due to noxious fumes	—	USA (1930s)
	white phosphorus*		dissolved in carbon disulphide		—	Germany, France, UK (1914)
	magnesium*		solid		—	Germany (1939)

Table 1 Chemical agents and their effects (*continued*)

Military category	Common/ code-name	Chemical name	Disseminated as	Effects	Lethal dosage†	Originated from
Anti-plant agents						
defoliants	2,4-D*	2,4-dichlorophenoxy-acetic acid	in diesel or kerosene mix		3500–35000	UK (1940–2)
	2,4,5-T*	2,4,5-trichlorophenoxy-acetic acid			35000–350000	USA (1940s)
	picloram*	4-amino-3,5,6-tri-chloropicolinic acid			—	USA (1960s)
anti-crop	cacodylic acid*	dimethylarsinic acid			100000	USA (1960s)
soil sterilants	bromacil*	5-bromo-3-sec-butyl-5-methyluracil			—	USA (1960s)
	monuron*	3-(p-chlorophenyl)-1,1-dimethylurea			—	USA (1960s)

*Stockpiled today

† Approximate dosage (milligram-minute/metre^3) of airborne agent likely to kill about 50 per cent of people exposed if unprotected. Oral exposure would reduce dosage dramatically (e.g. the lethal dose of VX taken orally = 0.3mg).

Sources: Based on data in SIPRI, *The Problem of Chemical and Biological Warfare, Vol. 1: The Rise of CB Weapons* (Stockholm, Almqvist & Wiksell, 1971) and SIPRI, *Chemical Disarmament: New Weapons for Old* (New York, Humanities Press, 1975).

Table 2 The lethality of chemical agents compared with some selected natural poisons

Chemical agent	*Name*	—————*Natural poison*————— *Source*
———	tetanus toxin	*Clostridium tetani* (bacteria)
———	botulinum toxin	*C. botulinum* (bacteria)
dioxin	tetrodotoxin spider venom toxin	puffer-fish black widow
VX soman	ricin tubocurarine	castor beans tube-curare arrow poison
sarin		
tabun	strychnine	*Strychnos* bark
hydrogen cyanide mustard gas Lewisite phosgene	nicotine rattlesnake venom	tobacco plants ———
chlorine	bee venom	honey bee

Note: The chemical agents and natural poisons are arranged in eight groups, the deadliest chemicals (those which are fatal in the smallest doses) occupying the top lines. Many of the natural poisons have been considered by the military as having potential in warfare (see chapters 3, 4 and 8).

Table 3 Pathogenic micro-organisms studied as potential biological warfare agents

Disease/military target and type	Causative agent	Death rate in untreated cases of natural disease (%)	Likely mode of dissemination	Remarks
Anti-personnel agents				
Viruses				
influenza		0–1	aerosol	
psittacosis	Chlamydia psittaci	10–100	aerosol	
Russian spring-summer encephalitis	RSSE virus	0–30	aerosol or tick vectors	standardised as BW agent by US*
yellow fever		4–100	aerosol or mosquito vectors	once infected, mosquito bite can cause disease
dengue fever		0–1	aerosol or mosquito vectors	
chikungunya		0–1	aerosol or mosquito vectors	
Venezuelan equine encephalomyelitis	VEE virus	0–2	aerosol or mosquito vectors	standardised as BW agent by US*
Rift Valley fever	RVF virus	0–1	aerosol or mosquito vectors	
smallpox	Variola	0–30	aerosol	Japanese tests on prisoners-of-war**
haemorrhagic dengue		0–5	aerosol or mosquito vectors	Japanese tests on prisoners-of-war**

Table 3 Pathogenic micro-organisms studied as potential biological warfare agents *(continued)*

Disease/military target and type	Causative agent	Death rate in untreated cases of natural disease (%)	Likely mode of dissemination	Remarks
Rickettsiae				
epidemic typhus		10–40	aerosol	Japanese tests on prisoners-of-war**
Rocky Mountain spotted fever		10–30	aerosol or tick vectors	
Q fever	*Coxiella burnetii*	1–4	aerosol	standardised as BW agent by US*
tsutsugamushi (scrub typhus)	*Rickettsia tsutsugamushi*		mite vectors	Japanese tests on prisoners-of-war**
Bacteria				
plague	*Pasteurella pestis*	30–100	aerosol or flea vectors	allegedly used by Japanese in China
anthrax	*Bacillus anthracis*	95–100	aerosol	standardised as BW agent by US*; intensively studied during Second World War by US and UK; Japanese tests on prisoners-of-war**

glanders	*Actinobacillus mallei*	90–100	aerosol	3200 inhaled bacteria may cause disease; Japanese tests on prisoners-of-war**
meliodosis	*Pseudomonas pseudomallei*	95–100	aerosol	
cholera	*Vibrio comma*	10–80	water contamination	like salmonella and shigella, allegedly used by saboteurs in China and Manchuria during late 1930s; Japanese tests on prisoners-of-war**
typhoid	*Salmonella typhosa*	4–20	aerosol or water or food contamination	100 ingested bacteria may cause disease; Japanese tests on prisoners-of-war**
dysentery	*Shigella* (species)	2–20	water or food contamination	oral infectious dose is about 5000 organisms in the case of *Sh. flexneri*; Japanese tests on prisoners-of-war*
tularaemia	*Francisella tularensis*	0–60	aerosol	standardised as BW agent by US;* Japanese tests on prisoners-of-war**

Table 3 Pathogenic micro-organisms studied as potential biological warfare agents *(continued)*

Disease/military target and type	Causative agent	Death rate in untreated cases of natural disease (%)	Likely mode of dissemination	Remarks
brucellosis	*Brucella* (species)	2–5	aerosol	1300 inhaled bacteria may cause disease; *B. suis* standardised as BW agent by US; intensively studied during Second World War by US and UK; Japanese tests on prisoners-of-war**
gas gangrene	*Clostridium perfringens*			Japanese tests on prisoners-of-war**
Fungi				
coccidioidomycosis	*Coccidioides immitis*	0–50	aerosol	
Anti-animal agents				
<u>Viruses</u>				
foot-and-mouth disease (cattle)	FMD virus	3–85	aerosol or water or food contamination	

rinderpest, or cattle plague		15–95	aerosol or water or food contamination	intensively studied during Second World War
vesicular stomatitis (cattle)		15–95	aerosol or water or food contamination	
Newcastle disease (poultry)		10–100	aerosol or water or food contamination	intensively studied during Second World War
fowl plague		90–100	aerosol or water or food contamination	a rare infection of chickens caused by a strain of influenza virus
African swine fever		95–100	aerosol or water or food contamination	
hog cholera		80–90	aerosol or water or food contamination	
Rickettsiae				
heart-water, or Veldt sickness (sheep and goats)	*Rickettsia ruminantium*	50–60	aerosol or tick vectors	
Fungi				
aspergillosis (poultry)	*Aspergillus fumigatus*	50–90	dust or food contamination	
lumpy-jaw (cattle)	*Actinomyces bovis*	50–90	food contamination	

Table 3 Pathogenic micro-organisms studied as potential biological warfare agents *(continued)*

Disease/military target and type	Causative agent	Death rate in untreated cases of natural disease (%)	Likely mode of dissemination	Remarks
Anti-plant agents				
Viruses				
tobacco mosaic				airborne transmission occurs naturally
sugar beet curly-top				vector-transmitted naturally (leafhoppers)
corn stunt				
hoja blanca (rice)				
Fiji disease (sugar cane)				vector-transmitted naturally (leafhoppers)
potato yellow dwarf				
Bacteria				
rice blight	*Xanthomonas oryzae*			
corn blight	*Pseudomonas alboprecipitans*			
sugar cane wilt (gumming disease)	*Xanthomonas vasculorum*			natural windborne transmission observed

Fungi

late blight of potato	*Phytophthora infestans*		aerosol or dust	responsible for the Irish potato famine of 1845–69
coffee rust	*Hemileia vastatrix*		aerosol or dust	responsible for the elimination of coffee from Ceylon in 1880s
maize rust	*Puccinia polysora*		aerosol or dust	transatlantic airborne transmission has been observed
powdery mildew of cereals	*Erysiphe graminis*		aerosol or dust	
black stem rust of cereals	*Puccinia graminis*	3–90	aerosol or dust	*P. graminis tritici* standardised as BW agent in US*
rice brown-spot disease	*Helminthosporium oryzae*		aerosol or dust	
rice blast	*Pyricularia oryzae*	50–90	aerosol or dust	standardised as BW agent in US*
stripe rust of cereals	*Puccinia glumarum*		aerosol or dust	

Notes:

*Biological agents which have been standardised or manufactured for inclusion in certain national chemical and biological weapons arsenals in the past.

**John W. Powell, 'Japan's Germ Warfare: The US Cover-up of a War Crime', *Bulletin of Concerned Asian Scholars*, vol. 12, no. 4, 1980.

Source: Based on SIPRI, *CB Weapons Today, Vol. 2: The Problems of Chemical and Biological Warfare* (Stockholm, Almqvist & Wiksell, 1972), pp. 38–41.

Table 4 Major toxic trichothecenes, their lethality and their origin

Major toxic trichothecenes*	LD50**	Producing species of Fusarium
(1) diacetoxyscirpenol (B-24 toxin)	23	F. tricinctum (= F. poae. sporotrichiodes), F. solani, F. lateritium, F. roseum (F. sambucinum, F. graminearum, F. equiseti, F. scirpi, Gibberella zeae, G. intricans), F. rigidiusculum
(2) HT-2 toxin	9	F. tricinctum, F. poae, F. solani, F. roseum (culmorum)
(3) T-2 toxin	5	F. tricinctum, F. roseum, F. lateritium, F. solani, Trichoderma viride, F. rigidiusculum
(4) neosolaninol	15	F. tricinctum, F. roseum, F. solani, F. rigidiusculum
(5) fusarenon-X	3	F. nivale, F. oxysporum, F. episphaeria (= F. aquaeductuum), F. merismoides
(6) nivalenol	4	F. nivale, F. episphaeria
(7) diacetylnivalenol	10	F. scirpi, F. nivale, F. equiseti, F. oxysporum
(8) dihydronivalenol DHN	15	F. nivale
(9) deoxynivalenol (RD-toxin or vomitoxin)	70	F. roseum

Notes:
*The fungal genus *Fusarium* is the principal source of trichothecene mycotoxins; however, it is not the only source. Other genera of fungi which produce trichothecenes are *Cephalosporium, Myrothecium, Trichoderma* and *Stachybotrys*.
**The dose (mg/kg body weight) that when injected into the body cavity of a group of mice would kill at least half of them.

Sources: Ueno, Y., Sato, N., Ishii, K., Sakai, K., Tsunoda, H., and Enomoto, M., 'Biological and chemical detection of trichothecene mycotoxins of fusarium species', *Applied Microbiology*, vol. 25, 1973, pp. 699–704; Uraguchi, K., and Yamazaki, M. (eds), *Toxicology: Biochemistry and Pathology of Mycotoxins* (New York, Wiley, 1978).

Table 5 The 1925 Geneva Protocol: signatories' (ratified) position on retaliation in kind

NATO		Warsaw Pact	
Retaliation reserved	*Retaliation not reserved*	*Retaliation reserved*	*Retaliation not reserved*
Belgium	Denmark	Bulgaria	East Germany
Canada	West Germany	Czechoslovakia	Hungary
France	Greece	Rumania	Poland
Netherlands*	Iceland	Soviet Union	
Portugal	Italy		
United Kingdom	Luxembourg		
United States*	Turkey		
	Norway		

*Reservation refers to chemical weapons only, not biological ones.

Notes

2. Chemical weapons

1. Stockholm International Peace Research Institute (SIPRI), *The Problem of Chemical and Biological Warfare, Vol. 4: CB Disarmament Negotiations 1920–1970* (Stockholm, Almqvist & Wiksell, 1971), pp.17–18.
2. SIPRI, *The Problem of Chemical and Biological Warfare, Vol. 1: The Rise of CB Weapons* (Stockholm, Almqvist & Wiksell, 1971), p.129.
3. Robert Harris and Jeremy Paxman, *A Higher Form of Killing* (London, Paladin, 1983), pp.43–4.
4. *CB Disarmament Negotiations 1920–1970*, pp.43–5.
5. *Ibid.* pp.341–8.
6. Julian Perry Robinson, 'The Changing Status of Chemical and Biological Warfare', in *World Armaments and Disarmament: SIPRI Yearbook 1982* (London, Taylor & Francis, 1982), pp.318–19.
7. *CB Disarmament Negotiations 1920–1970*, pp.175–89.
8. *Ibid.* pp.189–223.
9. *A Higher Form of Killing*, pp.55–6.
10. *The Rise of CB Weapons*, Chart 5.1.
11. *A Higher Form of Killing*, p.115.
12. R.V.Jones, letter to the *Daily Telegraph*, 28 April 1983.
13. *A Higher Form of Killing*, pp.107–36.
14. *Ibid.* p.139.
15. *The Rise of CB Weapons*, pp.74–5.
16. Russell Committee Against Chemical Weapons, *The Threat of Chemical Weapons* (Nottingham, Spokesman Pamphlet 78, Russell Press, 1982), p.21.
17. *CB Disarmament Negotiations 1920–1970*, pp.280–1.
18. 'The Changing Status of Chemical and Biological Warfare', pp.330–5.

19. *Europaische Wehrkunde*, vol. 27, 1978, pp.5–10.
20. 'The Changing Status of Chemical and Biological Warfare', pp.324–8.
21. *CB Disarmament Negotiations 1920–1970*, pp.196–223.
22. *Ibid.* pp.342–7.
23. 'The Changing Status of Chemical and Biological Warfare', and, also by Robinson, 'A Review of Developments during 1982 bearing on Chemical Warfare Disarmament', Tenth Pugwash CW Workshop, Geneva.
24. *Chemical and Engineering News*, 31 May 1982; *Daily Telegraph* (London), 18 March 1983.
25. 'The Changing Status of Chemical and Biological Warfare', pp.325–8.
26. SIPRI, *Chemical Disarmament: New Weapons for Old* (New York, Humanities Press, 1975), pp.94–9.
27. 'The Changing Status of Chemical and Biological Warfare', pp.348–9.
28. *Ibid.* p.331.
29. *CB Disarmament Negotiations 1920–1970*, pp.102–4.
30. *Employment of Chemical and Biological Agents*, field manual 3–10 (US Departments of the Army, Navy and Air Force, March 1966).
31. *Hearings before the Subcommittee on International Security and Scientific Affairs and on Asia and Pacific Affairs of the Committee on Foreign Affairs* (House of Representatives, Ninety-seventh Congress, 30 March 1982), p.21.
32. Chemical Corps Procurement Agency contract number CML-4564, let in 1952 to Shell Development Company.
33. 'The Changing Status of Chemical and Biological Warfare', p.326.
34. 'No One Told Them', *Newsweek*, 21 July 1975.
35. Alastair Hay, *Nature* (London), no. 302, 1983, pp.208–9.
36. *Ibid.*
37. Alastair Hay, *The Chemical Scythe: Lessons of 2,4,5-T and Dioxin* (New York, Plenum Press, 1982).
38. *Ibid.*
39. *Ibid.*
40. *A Higher Form of Killing*, p.196.
41. SIPRI, *Incendiary Weapons* (Massachusetts, MIT Press, 1975), pp.49–63.
42. L.F.Fieser, *The Scientific Method* (New York, Reinhold, 1964).
43. *Chemical Disarmament: New Weapons for Old*, pp.84–6.

3. Biological weapons

1. A.P.Ball and others, 'Human Botulism Caused by Clostridium Botulium.Type E: The Birmingham Outbreak', *Quarterly Journal of Medicine*, no. 48, 1979, pp.473–91.
2. Stockholm International Peace Research Institute (SIPRI), *The Problem of Chemical and Biological Warfare, Vol. 1: The Rise of CB Weapons* (Stockholm, Almqvist & Wiksell, 1971), p.215.
3. 'The Doctor and Disaster Medicine', part 2, *Clinical Medicine*, vol. 70, no. 1, 1963, pp.277–96.
4. World Health Organization (WHO), *Health Aspects of Chemical and Biological Warfare* (Geneva, WHO, 1970), p.69.
5. Robert Harris and Jeremy Paxman, *A Higher Form of Killing* (London, Chatto & Windus, 1982), pp.83 and 151.
6. Chiefs of Staff Committee, 'Potentialities of Weapons of War During the Next Ten Years' (Joint Technical Warfare Committee: note by joint secretaries), 12 November 1945.
7. 'Use of Bacteria in War', the *Times* (London), 4 January 1946.
8. Winston Churchill, personal minute to General Ismay (serial no. D162/4), 21 May 1944.
9. Julian Lewis, 'The Plan that Never Was: Churchill and the "Anthrax Bomb" ', *Encounter*, February 1982, pp.18–28.
10. Conference of the Committee on Disarmament (CCD/PV/458), 17 March 1970.
11. 'Military Considerations Affecting the Initiation of Chemical and Other Special Forms of Warfare (PRO, PREM 3/89), quoted in *A Higher Form of Killing*, p.133.
12. Conference on the Committee on Disarmament (CCD/PV/458), 17 March 1970.
13. 'The Plan that Never Was', pp.18–28.
14. 'Potentialities of Weapons of War during the Next Ten Years', 12 November 1945.
15. Minute by O.H.Wansbrough-Jones, 3 December 1945, in memo on 'Future Development of Biological Warfare' by ACIGS (W) War Office Chiefs of Staff Committee, Joint Technical Warfare Committee, 6 December 1945.
16. *A Higher Form of Killing*, pp.88–94.
17. PRO CAB 120/775, memo to Winston Churchill from General H.L. Ismay, 9 July 1942.
18. *Materials on the Trial of Former Servicemen of the Japanese Army Charged with Manufacturing and Employing Bacteriological Weapons* (Moscow, Foreign Languages Publishing House, 1950).

19. J.W.Powell, 'Japan's Germ Warfare: The US Cover-up of a War Crime', *Bulletin of Concerned Asian Scholars*, vol. 12, part 4, 1980, p.2–17.
20. R.Whymant, 'Hirohito Personally Approved Germ Warfare Unit', the *Guardian* (London), 17 September 1982.
21. 'Summary Report on BW Investigation', memo from Edwin V. Hill to General Alden C. Watt, Chief Chemical Corps (APO 500), 12 December 1947.
22. 'Hirohito Personally Approved Germ Warfare Unit', and R.Whymant, 'The Brutal Truth about Japan', the *Guardian*, 14 August 1982.
23. The *Guardian*, 14 August 1982. It has also been suggested that Emperor Hirohito of Japan personally approved the formation of a germ-warfare unit and that the work of the group was known only to him and to a handful of senior ministers and military commanders. Former members of Unit 731 are said to have testified that members of the imperial family visited Manchuria to inspect the unit ('Hirohito Personally Approved Germ Warfare Unit', the *Guardian*, 17 September 1982). However, the Japanese Embassy in London has denied the suggestion that Emperor Hirohito personally authorised the formation of Unit 731. According to an embassy official the emperor never had any interest in work of this nature (Akira Sugino, letter to the *Guardian*, 13 October 1982).
24. SIPRI, *The Problem of Chemical and Biological Warfare, Vol. 5: The Prevention of CBW* (Stockholm, Almqvist & Wiksell, 1971), p.238.
25. 'Japan's Germ Warfare: The US Cover-up of a War Crime'; *The Prevention of CBW*, p.238; and 'Report of the International Scientific Commission for the Investigation of the Facts Concerning Bacterial Warfare in Korea and China', *Chinese Medical Journal*, vol. 70, September–December 1952 (Peking).
26. SIPRI, *The Problem of Chemical and Biological Warfare, Vol. 6: Technical Aspects of Early Warning and Verification* (Stockholm, Almqvist & Wiksell, 1975), p.48.
27. SIPRI, *The Problem of Chemical and Biological Warfare, Vol. 2: CB Weapons Today* (Stockholm, Almqvist & Wiksell, 1973), p.79.
28. *A Higher Form of Killing*, p.155–9.
29. *Ibid.* pp.156–7.
30. *Health Aspects of Chemical and Biological Warfare*, p.68.
31. *Ibid.* p.73.
32. *Ibid.* pp.76–7.

33. *Ibid.* p.74.
34. Gwynne Roberts, 'The Deadly Legacy of Anthrax Island', *Sunday Times Magazine*, 15 February 1981; R.J.Manchee and others, 'Decontamination of *B.anthracis* on Gruinard Island', *Nature*, no. 303, 1983, pp.239–40.
35. *Health Aspects of Chemical and Biological Warfare*, p.62.
36. US Army Chemical Corps Historical Office, 'Summary of Major Events and Problems, United States Army Chemical Corps (U) Fiscal Year 1959' (Army Chemical Center, Maryland), January 1960. Previously secret document – now declassified.
37. *Health Aspects of Chemical and Biological Warfare*, p.82.
38. *Department of Defense Appropriations for 1970. Hearings before a Subcommittee on Appropriations* (US House of Representatives, Ninety-first Congress, First Session, Part 6), p.120.
39. *The Rise of CB Weapons*, p.65.
40. H.L.Craig and others, Preparations of Toxic Ricin, US Patent No. 3,060,165, 23 October 1962.
41. Record of interrogation of accused Mitomo Kazuo, 6 December 1949, in *Materials of the Trial of Former Servicemen of the Japanese Army Charged with Manufacturing and Employing Bacteriological Weapons*, pp.79–81.
42. *A Higher Form of Killing*, p.197, and Sterling Seagrave, *Yellow Rain* (New York, Evans, 1981), p.172.
43. *The Prevention of CBW*, p.142, and *Technical Aspects of Early Warning and Verification*, p.39.
44. *Technical Aspects of Early Warning and Verification*, p.67.
45. *CB Weapons Today*, pp.38–41.
46. *Health Aspects of Chemical and Biological Warfare*, p.102.
47. *The Prevention of CBW*, p.274.
48. Conference of the Committee on Disarmament, verbatim record (CCD/PV/458), 17 March 1970.
49. *CB Weapons Today*, p.128.
50. *The Rise of CB Weapons*, p.122.
51. Zhores Medvedev, 'The Great Russian Germ War Fiasco', *New Scientist*, 31 July 1980, pp.360–1.
52. *Ibid.*
53. *Report of Secretary of Defense Caspar W. Weinberger to the Congress on FY 1983 Budget, FY 1984 Authorization Request and FY 1983–1987 Defense Programs*, 8 February 1982.
54. Stephen Budiansky, 'US Looks to Biological Weapons', *Nature* (London), no. 297, 1982, pp.615–16.

55. Stephen Budiansky, 'No NIH Ban', *Nature* (London), no. 298, 1982, p.111.
56. *Ibid.*
57. Jonathan King, 'Biological Weapons: Present and Future', address to the American Association for the Advancement of Science, 1982.

4. Yellow rain

1. US State Department, *Fact Sheet on Chemical Warfare*, 21 September 1981.
2. Letter from the Permanent Representative of the Union of Soviet Socialist Republics to the Secretary General of the United Nations, 'Chemical and Bacteriological (Biological) Weapons', UN General Assembly document no. A/37/233, 21 May 1982; report of the Secretary General (UN), 'Chemical and Bacteriological (Biological) Weapons', United Nations General Assembly document no. A/37/259, 1 December 1982; Vietnam News Agency Report, 7 October 1981.
3. 'Haig Protestors in Berlin Clash', the *Guardian*, 14 September 1981.
4. *Fact Sheet on Chemical Warfare*.
5. Nicholas Cumming-Bruce, 'Kampucheans Treated for Poisoning', the *Guardian*, 24 March 1981, and 'Vietnam Used War Gas', the *Guardian*, 10 July 1982.
6. 'Poison Attacks on Laos Tribe', the *Guardian*, 8 January 1979.
7. Report of the Secretary General (UN), 'Chemical and Bacteriological (Biological) Weapons', United Nations General Assembly document no. A/36/613, 20 November 1981.
8. US State Department, *Report on Chemical Warfare*, 22 March 1982, and 'Chemical Warfare in Southeast Asia and Afghanistan: An Update', report from Secretary of State George P. Shultz, November 1982.
9. Sterling Seagrave, *Yellow Rain* (London, Abacus, 1982), pp.271–2.
10. S.Winchester, 'Poison "Proof" Under Fire', *Sunday Times*, 28 March 1982; editorial, 'Mycotoxins in South-East Asia?', *Nature* (London), no. 296, 1 April 1982, pp.379–80.
11. H.B.Scheifer, 'Study of the Possible Uses of Chemical Warfare Agents in South-East Asia', report to the Department of External Affairs, Canada, 1982.
12. H.Rose and S.P.R.Rose, 'Chemical Spraying as Reported by Refugees from South Vietnam', *Science*, no. 177, 1972, pp.710–12;

National Academy of Sciences (USA), 'Perceived Effects of Herbicides in the Highlands', in *The Effects of Herbicides in South Vietnam. Part A. Summary and Conclusions* (Washington, DC, National Academy of Sciences, 1974), pp.VII–58 – VII–66.

13. Report from Secretary of State George P. Shultz, November 1982.
14. Tregallas Williams (Australian High Commission), personal communication, 11 March 1983.
15. Peter Pringle, ' "Yellow Rain" Evidence Fake Scientists Say', the *Observer*, 6 March 1983.
16. S.Sukroongreung, S.Kritalugsana, C.Nilakul, K.Thakerngpol and P.Viryanonda, 'Examination of the Yellow Spot Samples Collected from Thailand Border Close to Cambodia', *Siraraj Hospital Gazette*, no. 34, 1982, pp.643–7; Mr Goodwin (UK Central Office of Information), personal communication, 10 March 1983.
17. Stephen Budiansky, 'Not Poison, But Pollen?', *Nature*, no. 302, 1982, pp.200–1.
18. O.A.Reinking and H.W.Wollenweber, 'Tropical Fusaria', *Philippine Journal of Science*, no. 32, 1928, pp.103–253.
19. Stephen Budiansky, 'Is Yellow Rain Simply Bees' Natural Excreta?', *Nature*, no. 303, 1983, p.3.
20. *Ibid.*
21. Francis Bugnicourt, 'Les Fusarium et Cylindrocarpond de l'Indochine', thesis presented to the Faculté des Sciences de L'université de Paris, 1939.
22. *Ban Chemical Weapons* (Moscow, Novosti Press Agency Publishing House, 1982), p.191.
23. Y.Ueno, N.Sato, K.Ishii, K.Sakai, H.Tsunoda and M.Enomoto, 'Biological and Chemical Detection of Trichothecene Mycotoxins of Fusarium Species', *Applied Microbiology*, no. 25, 1973, pp.699–704.
24. Grant Evans, *The Yellow Rain Makers* (London, Verso/New Left Books, 1983).
25. Report of the Secretary General (UN), 21 May 1982.
26. Personal communication from Professor Nicolai Antonov, Ho Chi Minh City, January 1983.
27. Peter Pringle, the *Observer*, 6 March 1983, and Alastair Hay, 'Yellow Rain: Act of Aggression or Act of God?', the *Guardian* (London), 17 March 1983.
28. 'Is Yellow Rain Simply Bees' Natural Excreta?', examination of yellow rain specimens received at MRL (Materials and Research Laboratory, Australia), April 1982; and 'Yellow Rain "Proof" Faked', the *Times* (London), 18 March 1983.

29. Press release, 'Former CIA Operative Charges Assassination Attempt, Suggests Fabrication of "Yellow Rain" Evidence', *Covert Action Information Bulletin*, 7 April 1982.
30. Kevin Cody, 'Spook or Spoof', *Easy Reader Reflections from the South Bay*, vol. 2, no. 34, 15 April 1982.
31. Nicholas Cumming-Bruce, 'Colonel's Surrender Ends Laos Hunt for POWs', the *Guardian* (London), 2 March 1982.
32. Personal communication from Nicolai Antonov, January 1983.
33. 'Colonel's Surrender Ends Laos Hunt for POWs'.
34. Matthew Meselson, personal communication, 22 April 1982.
35. David Dickinson, 'Biological Warfare: Soviet Use', *Nature*, no. 296, 1982, pp.281–2.
36. B.B.Jarvis, J.O.Midiwo, D.Tuthill and G.A.Bean, 'Interaction between the Antibiotic Trichothecenes and the Higher Plant *Baccharis megapotamica*', *Science*, no. 214, 1982, pp.460–2.
37. R.J.Cole and R.H.Cox, 'The Trichothecenes', in *Handbook of Toxic Fungal Metabolites* (New York, Academic Press, 1981), p.153.
38. Personal interview with Dr Amos Townsend, Bangkok, 4 January 1983.

5. Chemical and biological warfare: military scenarios

1. Stockholm International Peace Research Institute (SIPRI), *The Problems of Chemical and Biological Warfare*, vol. 2: *CB Weapons Today* (Stockholm, Almqvist & Wiksell, 1973), p.142.
2. Department of the Army, *Employment of Chemical Agents*, field manual FM3-10 (Departments of the Army, Navy and Air Force), November 1966.
3. Amoretta M. Hoeber and J.D.Douglas, Jnr, 'The Neglected Threat of Chemical Warfare', *International Security*, vol. 3, 1978, pp.55–82.
4. *CB Weapons Today*, p.143.
5. Jean Meyer, 'Starvation as a Weapon – Herbicides in Vietnam', *Scientist and Citizen*, no. 9, 1967, pp.115–21.
6. A.H.Westing, 'The Environmental Aftermath of Warfare in Vietnam', in *World Armaments and Disarmament, SIPRI Yearbook 1982* (London, Taylor & Francis, 1982), pp.363–89.
7. 'The Neglected Threat of Chemical Warfare'.
8. *CB Weapons Today*, p.144.
9. Matthew Meselson and Julian Perry Robinson, 'Chemical Warfare and Chemical Disarmament', *Scientific American*, no. 242, 1980, pp.24–43.

10. *CB Weapons Today*, p.145.
11. *Ibid.* p.146.
12. *Ibid.*
13. J.B.Nielands, 'Gas Warfare in Vietnam in Perspective', in *Harvest of Death* (London, Collier Macmillan, 1972), pp.3–101.
14. *Employment of Chemical Agents*, field manual FM3–10.
15. *CB Weapons Today*, p.150.
16. 'Chemical Warfare and Chemical Disarmament'.
17. *Ibid.*
18. *Ibid.*
19. *Ibid.*
20. John Erickson, 'The Soviet Union's Growing Arsenal of Chemical Warfare', *Strategic Review*, fall 1979, pp.63–71.
21. G.M.Lovelace, 'Chemical Warfare', *NATO's Fifteen Nations*, December 1981–January 1982, pp.54–6.
22. 'Chemical Warfare and Chemical Disarmament'.
23. World Health Organization (WHO), *Health Aspects of Chemical and Biological Weapons* (Geneva, WHO, 1970), p.103.
24. *Ibid.* p.81.
25. *Ibid.* pp.98–9.
26. *Ibid.* p.116.
27. *Ibid.* p.124.
28. *CB Weapons Today*, p.151.
29. *Ibid.* p.153.
30. 'Chemical Warfare and Chemical Disarmament'.
31. *Employment of Chemical Agents*, field manual FM3–10.

6. The law

1. Stockholm International Peace Research Institute (SIPRI), *The Problem of Chemical and Biological Warfare, Vol. 3: CBW and the Law of War* (Stockholm, Almqvist & Wiksell, 1973), p.151.
2. *Ibid.* p.152.
3. *Ibid.* p.155.
4. Arthur Westing, 'Chemical and Biological Weapons: Past and Present', *Peace and the Sciences*, no. 3, 1982, pp.25–37.
5. Russell Committee Against Chemical Weapons, *The Threat of Chemical Weapons* (Nottingham, Spokesman Pamphlet 78, Russell Press, 1982).
6. *CBW and the Law of War*, p.82.

7. SIPRI, *The Problem of Chemical and Biological Warfare, Vol. 1: The Rise of Chemical and Biological Weapons* (Stockholm, Almqvist & Wiksell, 1971), pp.142–6.
8. *Ibid*. pp.147–52.
9. Alastair Hay, *The Chemical Scythe: Lessons of 2,4,5-T and Dioxin* (New York, Plenum Press, 1982), pp.147–85.
10. R.Mikulak, 'Defence Planning for Chemical Warfare', in *Chemical Weapons and Chemical Arms Control* (Washington, DC, Carnegie Endowment for International Peace, 1978), p.13.
11. SIPRI, *The Problem of Chemical and Biological Warfare, Vol. 5: The Prevention of CBW* (Stockholm, Almqvist & Wiksell, 1971), pp.45–6.
12. *CBW and the Law of War*, p.57.
13. *Ibid*. pp.167–9.
14. *The Threat of Chemical Weapons*.
15. *Ibid*. pp.172–7.
16. Foreign and Commonwealth Office, *Arms Control and Disarmament*, no. 11, February 1982, p.3.
17. *The Threat of Chemical Weapons*.
18. Max Kempelman, text of remarks by the head of the US delegation to the CSCE Review Meeting in Madrid on 16 February 1982 (International Communication Agency, US Embassy, London); Foreign and Commonwealth Office, 'Peace and Disarmament: A Short Guide to British Government Policy', *Arms Control and Disarmament*, January 1982.
19. Max Kempelman, *op. cit*.
20. 'Peace and Disarmament: A Short Guide to British Government Policy'.
21. SIPRI, *Chemical Weapons: Destruction and Conversion* (London, Taylor & Francis, 1980), pp.165–8.
22. Soviet Union Chemical Warfare Convention Proposals, New York, 18 June 1982; also UN General Assembly document no. A/S–12A/C1/12, 17 June 1982.
23. *The Threat of Chemical Weapons*.
24. *The Prevention of CBW*, p.119.
25. Congressional Report, 22 July 1982.
26. *The Threat of Chemical Weapons*.
27. National Security Council, *Fact Sheet on Chemical Weapons*, 8 February 1982.
28. Lt Col G.M.Lovelace, 'Chemical Warfare', *NATO's Fifteen Nations*, December 1981–January 1982, pp.54–6.
29. Lois R. Ember, 'Army Seeks to Make Nerve Gas Chemicals',

Chemical and Engineering News, vol. 60, no. 34, 1982, pp.32–4.

30. Committee on Disarmament document no. CD/343, 10 February 1983; United States of America, 'United States Detailed Views on the Contents of a Chemical Weapons Ban'.
31. 'Soviet Union Chemical Warfare Convention Proposals'.
32. 'United States Detailed Views on the Contents of a Chemical Weapons Ban'.
33. Committee on Disarmament document no. CD/342, 8 February 1983. 'Report of the Ad Hoc Working Group on Chemical Weapons on its Work Done during the Period 17–28 January 1983'.
34. Speech by the Rt Hon. Douglas Hurd, CBE MP, to the Committee on Disarmament on Thursday 10 March 1983, Foreign and Commonwealth Office.
35. 'Verification of Non-production of Chemical Weapons', UK submission to Committee on Disarmament, 10 March 1983.
36. *Common Security: a Programme for Disarmament. Report of the Commission under the chairmanship of Swedish premier Olaf Palme* (London, Pan Books, 1982).
37. 'Political Declaration of the Warsaw Treaty Member States', Prague, 6 January 1983.

7. Hands across the sea: the UK–USA alliance

1. R.Harris and J.Paxman, *A Higher Form of Killing* (London, Paladin, 1983), p.96.
2. *Ibid*. p.155.
3. Russell Committee Against Chemical Weapons, *The Threat of Chemical Weapons* (Nottingham, Spokesman Pamphlet 78, Russell Press, 1982), p.21.
4. Stockholm International Peace Research Institute (SIPRI), *The Problem of Chemical and Biological Warfare, Vol. 1: Biological Warfare* (Stockholm, Almqvist & Wiksell, 1971), p.277.
5. Personal communication from Julian Perry Robinson.
6. B.Hayhoe, Parliamentary Debates, House of Commons, *Hansard*, vol. 968, 12 June 1979, col.158.
7. F.Pym, *ibid*. vol. 986, 17 June 1980, col.1326; M.Thatcher, *ibid.*, col.1334.
8. H.Stanhope, the *Times* (London), 3 April 1980, p.1.
9. The *Times* (London), 3 June 1980, p.1.
10. F.Emery, the *Times* (London), 3 June 1980, p.1.

11. R.Norton-Taylor, the *Guardian* (London), 18 December 1980, p.11.
12. B.Hayhoe, Parliamentary Debates, House of Commons, *Hansard*, vol. 983, 28 April 1980, cols.1109–10.
13. D.Fairhall, the *Guardian* (London), 30 December 1981, p.1.
14. Julian Perry Robinson, in 'The Changing Status of Chemical and Biological Warfare', *World Armaments and Disarmament: SIPRI Yearbook 1982* (London, Taylor & Francis, 1982), pp.348–9.
15. *Ibid.*
16. F.Pym, Parliamentary Debates, House of Commons, *Hansard*, vol. 991, 7 November 1980, cols.692–3.
17. D.Campbell, the *Observer* (London), 17 April 1983, p.1.
18. Reported in the *Times* (London), 30 September 1982.

8. Developments in chemical and biological weapons

1. The *Times* (London), 10 and 26 September 1981.
2. It is not intended to give a detailed description of techniques that have been developed to make a cell produce a foreign protein. For a good account see R.Gibson, 'Genetic Manipulation, Principles and Practice', *Biologist*, no. 29, 1982, pp.191–7.
3. *Report of the Working Party on the Experimental Manipulation of the Genetic Composition of Micro-organisms*, cmnd.5880 (London, HMSO, 1975), p.9.
4. *Federal Register*, 48, 1983, pp.1156–8.
5. S.Wright and R.Sinsheimer, 'The Fourth Horseman: Recombinant DNA Technology and Biological Warfare', *Bulletin of the Atomic Scientists* (in press).
6. For a complete list, see *ibid.* Table 1.
7. *Ibid.*
8. Stephanie Yanchinski, 'Genetic Engineers Campaign Against Gene Warfare', *New Scientist*, vol. 94, 1982, p.827.
9. Stephen Budiansky, 'US Looks to Biological Weapons', *Nature*, no. 298, 1982.
10. Julian Perry Robinson, 'A Review of Developments during 1982 bearing on CW Disarmament', background paper to Tenth Pugwash CW Workshop (Geneva).
11. P.Pringle, *Defence Week*, 22 February 1982, pp.1 and 4.
12. US Army Research and Development Command, laboratory posture report F7–77.
13. US Army Armament Research and Development Command, chemical systems laboratory, 10 October 1980.

Further reading

G.Evans, *The Yellow Rain Makers* (London, Verso/New Left Books, 1983), paperback.

R.Harris and J.Paxman, *A Higher Form of Killing* (London, Paladin, 1983), paperback.

A.Hay, *The Chemical Scythe* (New York, Plenum Press, 1982).

M.Meselson and J. Perry Robinson, 'Chemical Warfare and Chemical Disarmament', *Scientific American*, April 1980.

Russell Committee Against Chemical Weapons, *The Threat of Chemical Weapons* (Nottingham, Spokesman Pamphlet 78, Russell Press, 1982).

S.Seagrave, *Yellow Rain* (London, Sphere Books, 1982), paperback.

E.Sigmund, *Rage Against the Dying* (London, Pluto Press, 1980), paperback.

P.Watson, *War on the Mind* (London, Hutchinson, 1979).

Index